# In Your Hands

### THE POWER OF THE DADDY/DAUGHTER RELATIONSHIP

# In Your Hands

THE POWER OF THE DADDY/DAUGHTER RELATIONSHIP

BY

ONEDIA N. GAGE, PH. D., CLC

# LIBRARY OF CONGRESS

In Your Hands:
The Power of the Daddy/Daughter Relationship

All Rights Reserved © 2022
Onedia N. Gage, Ph. D., CLC

No part of this book may be reproduced or transmitted in
Any form or by any means, graphic, electronic, or mechanical,
Including photocopying, recording, taping, or by any
Information storage or retrieval system, without the
Permission in writing from the publisher.

Purple Ink, Inc. Press

For Information address:
Purple Ink, Inc.
10223 Broadway St., P292
Pearland, TX 77584
www.purpleink.net ♦ onediagage@purpleink.net

Onedia Gage Ministries

www.onediagage.com ♦ onediagage@onediagage.com

ISBN:
978-1-939119-08-7

Printed in the United States

*In Your Hands*

OTHER BOOKS BY
# ONEDIA N. GAGE, PH. D.

Are You Ready for 9th Grade . . . Again? A Family's Guide to Success
As We Grow Together Daily Devotional for Expectant Couples
As We Grow Together Prayer Journal for Expectant Couples
As We Grow Together Bible Study: Her Workbook
As We Grow Together Bible Study: His Workbook
The Best 40 Days of My Life: A Journey of Spiritual Renewal
The Blue Print: Poetry for the Soul
From Fat to Fit in 90 Days: A Fitness Journal
From Two to One: The Notebook for the Christian Couple
Hannah's Voice: Powerful Lessons in Prayer
The Heart of a Woman: The Depth of Her Spirit (Poetry)
Her Story The Legacy of Her Fight: The Bible Study
Her Story The Legacy of Her Fight: The Devotional
Her Story The Legacy of Her Fight: The Legacy Journal
Her Story The Legacy of Her Fight: Prayers and Journal
I Am.: 90 Days of Powerful Words: Affirmation and Advice for Girls
ILY! A Mother Daughter Relationship Workbook
In Her Own Words: Notebook for the Christian Woman
In 90 Days: What Will You Do?
In Purple Ink: Poetry for the Spirit
Intensive Couples Retreat: Her Workbook
Intensive Couples Retreat: His Workbook
Living A Whole Life: Sermons Which Prompt, Provoke, and Provide Life
Love Letters to God from a Teenage Girl
The Measure of a Woman: The Details of Her Soul
The Notebook: For Me, About Me, By Me
The Notebook for the Christian Teen
On This Journey Daily Devotional for Young People
On This Journey Prayer Journal for Young People
On This Journey Prayer Journal for Young People, Vol. 2
One Day More Than We Deserve Prayer Journal for the Growing Christian
Promises, Promises: A Novel
Queen in the Making: 30 Week Bible Study for Teen Girls
Queen in the Making: 30 Week Bible Study for Teen Girls Leader's Guide
There's a Queen Within: Her Journey to Self—Worth
She Spoke Volumes . . . And Then Some
Six Months of Solitude: The Sanctity of Singleness Notebook
Six Months of Solitude: The Sanctity of Singleness Prayers and Journal
Tools for These Times: Timely Sermons for Uncertain Times

What Did You Say? Affirmations. Encouragement. Motivation.
With An Anointed Voice: The Power of Prayer
A Woman Like Me: A Bible Study
A Woman Like Me: A Daily Devotional
A Woman Like Me: A Sermonic Study
Yielded and Submitted: A Woman's Journey for a Life Dedicated to God
Yielded and Submitted: A Woman's Journey for a Life Dedicated to God An Intimate Study
Yielded and Submitted: A Woman's Journey for a Life Dedicated to God Prayers and Journal

## The Nehemiah Character Series

Nehemiah and His Basketball
Nehemiah and His Big Sister
Nehemiah and His Bike
Nehemiah and His Flag Football Team
Nehemiah and His Football
Nehemiah and His Golf Clubs
Nehemiah and Math
Nehemiah and the Bully
Nehemiah and the Busy Day
Nehemiah and the Class Field Trip
Nehemiah and the Substitute for the Substitute
Nehemiah Can Swim
Nehemiah Found the Mud
Nehemiah Reads to Mommy
Nehemiah Writes Just Like Mommy
Nehemiah, the Hot Dog, and the Broccoli
Nehemiah's Family Vacation
Nehemiah's Favorite Teacher Returns to School
Nehemiah's First Day of School
Nehemiah's Sister Moved
Nehemiah's Visit to the Hospital

*In Your Hands*

## Dedication

### To All Dads

I write this because you need to be notified. This is your notice: I am going to speak—boldly—with authority, challenging you to be a better father AND daddy.

There is a difference!

### To All Daughters

Give him a chance to learn what he needs to do for you. Offer him some grace so that he can take action. Do your part to make the relationship work.

### Jordan Dominique Nicole

I love you!

I apologize.

### Sam Gage, Jr.

"What do you know good?"

I hope that I have made you proud. I miss you dearly.

### Cornelius D. Carroll, !

"How's the world treating you?"

I still need to talk to you. I am sorry that I was not there at the end.

*In Your Hands*

Daddy,

As a little girl, I always wanted to be the apple of your eye. I wanted all of your attention. I wanted all of your approval. As your little girl, I want you to love me unconditionally. I want you to love me the way I need to be loved.

I need your protection from hurt, pain, and others. Sometimes, I need your protection from myself and you and other family members.

I need your wisdom for my future so that we do not share similar mistakes. I need your wisdom to make better choices and decisions. I need your wisdom to show me that your experiences are for my benefit.

I need your education so that I will strive for my very best mind. You have lessons to teach me that only you can and for which you are completely responsible.

I need your heart with the genuine care and compassion that I need so I can care for others as well. This care and concern are what I need to relate to others.

I need access to your heart, mind, and soul transparently—so transparent that I can use what I see and am exposed to you and your life.

I need you to be present in my life—physically, emotionally, and spiritually. I need you engaged in my life. You have to be committed to my growth, development, and my enlightenment.

I need YOU! I need you, Daddy! I need you to do the job God assigned you to do! You cannot quit and you cannot take a break! This is your JOB—not someone else's! Be present to do your job!

The risk of you not doing your job is that I become someone you do not understand, that I struggle to understand the man in my life, and that I seek ways to manage my self-esteem that may result in neither of you us being proud.

I am worth whatever it takes for you to be my dad! I love you! I want you to love me! Your relationship impacts every relationship in my life—from God to my grandchildren.

Please stay engaged.

From a Daughter Currently Without a Dad!

Onedia N. Gage

## WHY DID I WRITE THIS BOOK?

Dads need some help. This is not a criticism. This is an observation. This observation is based on my experiences with Dads. Some of those experiences have been good and some have been sad. The commonality is that those dads do not know how powerful the daddy-daughter relationship is. When I speak to dads about their daughters, they are in a place of helplessness because she has pushed all of their limits. He no longer knows what to do with his daughter because he still sees her as the baby or toddler or eight-year-old she once was. He thought she was going to stay little. He lost track of time. Those days passed too quickly.

Dads, this is a hard time. She is growing. She growing physically. She is growing up. She talks to you with an unexpected intellect. She has unexpected knowledge and logic.

I write you to help: my help is not necessarily different from what you may have heard but you can hear me because I am not her mother or any other relative that has previously said this. I will share the "inside scoop."

I am prepared for your fatherly success!

I need you to be successful for her!

Your relationship makes a HUGE difference in her life. In every aspect.

I am here to advocate for both of you! I have seen the results of my work and investment!

*In Your Hands*

## What You Are to Do with This Information:

As her dad, you have a unique job. This book is designed to help you to do your job. This book is going to reveal ways to do that job, what it means to her in her life and what happens when it does not.

I will give you everything I know to make you successful. I need you both successful. I need her successful because I teach this girl, I tutor this girl, I mentor this girl, and I employ this girl.

I am talking because no one else has. My transparency is going to help your relationship and her life.

Use this information. Share this information. Take action so that she can have a different future.

# For All Dads: Tell Her the Truth

Tell her truth

How to take care of a man

How to kiss that same man

How to love that man

Authentically

Tell her why you love her mother

And never leave her mother

Correct the misconception

Of her reality

Give her a better view of her reality

She lives there but has no access

Tell her truth

About true love

Tell her how to arrive there

Give her the scoop

Solve the mystery of you

Her decisions are based on what she doesn't know

Tell her the truth

About what she doesn't know

Give her more tools

Enhance her self-esteem

Boost her self-confidence

Give her parts of you

She's never had

Be the dad of her dreams

Be the consultant for her decisions

Be the truth

Give her access to your heart

Give her inroads to your soul

Be her answer

Show her how to relax in the arms of a man

Show her how to argue with a man and

Never lose her cool

Show her how to her type

Whether type A or not

Remind her that type A is not required

Tell her how to be herself

Help her find who that is

With and without her baby, her mother, her brother

Give her problems to solve

Starting with her own

Give her projects to complete

Starting with herself

Give the understanding of how you love me

Inside and out

You control that definition and how she defines herself

*In Your Hands*

Help her understand her love language

Help her understand your language

Help her understand your behavior

Be the man in her life

Show her how to keep a man

Show her how to attract a man like you

Or a man you like

Help her understand those sacrifices

You made for her

Tell her the truth

The truth you have never shared

The truth she needs to get out of her rut

Equip her for her future

Redefine her definition of herself

Disconnect and unrelate that definition to her failures of her past

Start answering the why's before she asks

Show her how to survive the p---- war she started

Show her what it takes to have each one of her dreams

Show her how to be a parent

Take her by the hand and show her

Show her a man that is on her side

Help her with her definitions

Of success, love, happiness, joy, peace

Tell her what it means to fall in love

Stop speaking metaphorically

*The Power of the Daddy/Daughter Relationship*

Tell her the why behind your actions

You assume she understands what you do and

What she sees

What about what she doesn't see

What about when she doesn't understand

Show her the end game

Be her best friend

Furnish her a safe place

She's acting out to get your attention

She's calling for you through her behavior

## Table of Contents

| | |
|---|---|
| Letters | 11 |
| Poem: "For All Dads: Tell Her the Truth" | 17 |
| Your Job as Dad | 23 |
| Father's Letter to His Daughters: Gary Flenoy | 42 |
| Her Job as a Daughter | 43 |
| Communication | 49 |
| Mental Landmines | 55 |
| The Metaphorical Lifestyle Mistake | 59 |
| Listen | 63 |
| Her Example—Role Model | 65 |
| Father's Letter to His Daughters: Rev. Aaron Dallas, Sr. | 68 |
| Questions | 71 |
| Answers | 73 |
| The Leaning Tower of Pisa | 75 |
| Your Vision of Her | 77 |
| Your Protection of Her—Your Shotgun | 81 |
| Perfect Relationship by Design | 83 |
| Who is She? | 85 |
| Who are You? | 87 |
| Team Daddy/Daughter | 89 |
| Your Relationship with Her Mother | 91 |
| Her Relationship with Her Mother | 93 |

| | |
|---|---|
| Her Self-Esteem | 95 |
| Father's Letter to His Daughters: Kyron J. Gage, Sr. | 126 |
| Gumbo | 127 |
| What Dad Does This Well? | 128 |
| The Schedule | 129 |
| Your Other Relationships | 130 |
| In Your Hands | 131 |
| Acknowledgements | 133 |
| About the Daughter | 135 |

*In Your Hands*

# YOUR JOB AS HER DAD

**DEFINITION OF DADDY AND FATHER**

In this community, we use the terms dad, daddy, and father interchangeably. There is an idea that sometimes those words are different as the reflection of the relationship. Father carries with it the respect and reverence but could include an uncomfortable distance between the father and the daughter.

As a daughter, we use the descriptive name that you uphold because of your words and deeds. Daddy is used as an affectionate measure to communicate our love and request your attention and "spoiling."

The definition she has for you is driven by you. You decide how that definition is established and maintained.

How will you establish that definition? How will you maintain that definition?

**WANTED!**

A good dad—a father—who will love her. A good dad who will teach her to walk, help her up when she falls, teach her to ride her bike, and show her how to fish, barbecue, and play golf. A dad who would teach her how to win and more importantly, how to lose. A dad who will answer her endless questions and give her bountiful wisdom. A dad that will love her unconditionally, protect her from people, places, and things that will hurt and try to defeat her, even if it is protection from herself or you. A dad who considers her heart and its needs. A dad who will discipline her with love and leadership, kindness and compassion. A dad who will feed her spiritually. A dad who will pray for her life. A dad who will show her how to accept a husband. A dad who will help her get along with her mother. A dad who will be her counselor. A dad who will compliment her often. A dad who will buy her first dozen long stem red roses. A good dad—wanted!

Please email your daughter and let her know that you are ready for your job. She will accept your commitment unconditionally because she wants it so badly! No one can take your place.

I want you to accept your job because it affects the rest of your life.

**DESCRIPTION OF A GREAT DAD.**

God gives leadership and defines and illustrates the portrait of a dad. As we compare the word of God and God's behavior to what we normally see from average dads, even from excellent dads, we find that we still fall short of His excellence and expectations.

In the description of a great dad, we will start with the attributes and characteristics that dads should embody. Next, we will consider the mismeasurement the world imposes on dads. Concluding, we will remind all dads of your calling.

God is a Dad! God teaches! God teaches His children about the word of God, the characteristics of Himself, and the importance of character for the children. As God continues to show Himself to us, He repeatedly explains and demonstrates His Fatherhood to us.

God fathered all of us. He is here—available for us. He does not lie to us. He has plans for us. He does not disappear. He lets us exercise a certain amount of free will. He disciplines us to His glory. He loves us unconditionally. He provides for us. He has His best in mind for us. He continuously communicates with us. He sent His Son to die for our sins and save our lives.

Yes, I know that you are not God—not even close. But let us start with what you can do. Love. Forgiveness. Promises. Provisions. Wisdom. Vision. Communication. Discipline. Work ethic. Truth. Worship. Educate. Time. Tenderness. More: God. Pray. Study. Fast.

**LOVE.**

Daddys offer unconditional love. As a daddy, you are to actively love your child, especially your daughter. You are her definition of a man—a good man, a great man, or a sorry man. She uses your model to decide how to love others, especially the men in her life. You are the best way for her to decide who to select as a man. If you don't like her choice, consider your contribution to that poor choice. You have the biggest influence over that.

Unconditional love is rare even from parents. How do you do it? Love is a verb. What do you do to show your love? Some key elements factor into unconditional love for your daughter: 'Does my Dad keep his word? Does my dad show up to my events? Is he invested in my life at a level that lets me know that he is concerned about me? Does my Dad give me wise, helpful, and healthy information? When he does disappoint, does he own his behavior or does he discount his role and impact? Does he put other people in front of me? Does he have a life balance that gives me the time that I need? Do I have his attention upon request?'

Remember that the grade you receive as an unconditionally, loving father is from her—your daughter. She is your grader. What you think that she should accept as your best may earn you an F, even though you believe that you should get an A.

Love is being there. Does she have events and occasions which require your presence? Do you go to her life events? Please understand that if you don't ever go to those events, your influence is consistently diminishing each time you are absent.

Love is keeping your word. If you say something, that should be able to be counted on. If you have to add, 'I promise,' so that you can be held accountable for your words, then your words are only suggestions, so she listens with that same attitude. She listens to you with disbelief—one that you do not pay attention to. Your word should be one of her resources, one of authority in her life, and a foundational provision. When your word no longer means anything to her because you don't keep your word, what are you going to do? How are you going to feel when you lose that influence over her life and her actions?

If you don't have any additional influence or power over her with your words, then you are heard at the same level as her friends and Google. Don't you want to be more sought after than her friends and Google? To do that, your word should mean something.

Love is an example. Be her example of what to do, how to behave, how to forgive, how to parent, and how to love. Who are you as an example? Can she depend on you as an example? Are you dependable? Reliable? Do you behave well? Do you love well?

One of the parental report cards we need to be careful of or we will surely fail is when we expect something of our children that we have not done or cannot do or something we have not taught them. If you expect her to be educated, then so should you. If you don't want her to be drunk, publicly or privately, then you should not be drunk either. If you don't want her to be labeled a whore or slut, then you should halt your womanizing. If you want her treated well, then you should treat other women well. Don't expect or ask for anything that may cause her to say, "But Daddy you do it!" That cold water and slap in the face will hurt. Fix your stuff so that you can be a man—her father—whom she respects.

You want her respect. You feel that you deserve her respect. You feel that you deserve her respect no matter what has ever happened or whatever has taken place, while she may not feel that you deserve that respect. She may not feel as if you should be respected. This will be evident in her walk and her words. You will know.

What happens when you do fail her? Word to a wise father: OWN YOUR ERROR. If you need to fail her, own it! Do not make additional excuses. Own it. Be held accountable. Be honest about why you had to disappoint her. Be forthcoming—do not make her ask you why you didn't show up. How often do you fail her? Limit that. You have no idea of how it feels to look for you, especially since you said you would be there, and then you do not show up. Further, it is embarrassing to say 'my daddy is coming' but you fail to show up. It's like being the last kid to be picked up at school. One too many of those embarrassing moments and she will never mention anything else that you say. Stop failing her.

## FORGIVENESS.

Teach her to forgive. Greatness will forgive. Forgive yourself. Forgive her mother. Remind her to forgive herself. Forgive her. Make sure that she can forgive you.

Forgiveness frees your soul. Forgiveness keeps you focused on the purposes you have. Harboring unforgiveness hardens her heart and yours. Teach her to forgive by forgiving. Then you can hold her accountable for forgiveness. Remember that you have to be THE example.

## PROMISES.

The world makes promises to her that she will never receive. You should not fit into that category. She should be able to count on your word. Your word and your promises should be the same. If you have to include 'I promise' in your statement, then you need to reconsider how you make promises and statements.

She should be able to count on your word. That will translate into respect for you. She should not have to wonder 'will he be where he said he would' or 'do what he said he would.'

Please do not put yourself in a position where she never believes you and you have no influence in her life.

*In Your Hands*

## PROVISION.

Provision is a big word—encompassing lots of areas of her life. One provision is financially providing. Not too mysterious. Are you her financial resource? If you are not helping her financially then who is? What does 'that' cost her?

The second provision includes accommodations. A little more difficult to comprehend and carry out. This is best shown through illustration. You are remarried. She wants to spend some time with you. She wants to go somewhere on the same night as date night with your wife. How do you make that happen without sacrificing either woman's feelings? You may not be able to but how you handle this is the difference in her reaching out again. Did you make provisions for her to see you? Did she feel important in the decision you made? Did she feel like you chose your wife over her?

This is hard to do at times. It requires all of your efforts but is worth it. DAILY. Vision and planning is the only way to make that work.

## WISDOM.

Wisdom is the combination of knowledge and experience. Information developed from lessons you have learned that she should not have to re-learn. Wisdom is knowing to share your knowledge and experience, coupled with the influence that ensures that she listens and heeds your advice.

Listen to her. Listen. Listen with an open mind. Listen. Listen without judgment. Listen. Listen before speaking. Listen. Listen before asking questions. Listen. Listen without prejudice. Listen. Listen without trying to fix it. Listen.

Teach her how to solve her own problems. Not because you are not able to or not willing to but because one day you will leave this Earth and she will need to know how to come to her rescue.

In the meantime, you have a lot to teach her. Fatherhood is a full—time job. Maybe you don't see her daily but you can teach her daily. Technology allows for options via text, email, or other software and applications or apps. Daily you can share wisdom and teach life lessons. Daily you can express your love. Never stop sharing. Do not underestimate your influence. Never reduce your influence by opting out of sharing.

**VISION.**

Vision is defined as future planning and a future thought process. Sharing your vision for her is first. What did you have in mind for her? What did you have planned for her? Why? If she is off track, how do you help her get back on track?

Do you influence this area? How does she grade your life? Will she listen and accept your suggestions about her life? Are you ever going to ask her for excellence but she responds that you have never done anything of significance? Dad, we need you to adjust your life in a manner that she is not compelled to respond in such a manner.

## COMMUNICATION.

Your communication influences her decisions, her communication, her perception, and her growth. Do everything in your power to keep your status as her SOURCE for information. You are in competition with her friends, other family members, and the internet.

Communication. Be her source. Be her Source. Plan your communication. Be a man of your word. Your word should be dependable without the word PROMISE. Your communication should not be dependent on the word or concept of promise.

Be honest. Be transparent. Be authentic. Be present. Be considerate. Live by the priorities you expect of her. Share wise learnings. Share stories. Share your philosophy. Teach her about life—that's your job. Keep her informed. What she does not know is your responsibility. What she knows is your responsibility. Don't rely on metaphors and other poetic devices. Direct is the best approach. She does not have the life experience to read between your lines. She should not have to do so either. This is daddy-daughter. She is privileged with all of your experience and knowledge and wisdom.

Do not assume that she understands your message. Check for her understanding. Ask her if she has any questions. Encourage her to share her fears and any misunderstandings.

Make your communication clear, consistent, and conventional. Separate yourself from the 'competition.' Be her Dad. She gets one and it is YOU!

**DISCIPLINE.**

You are still her dad. Discipline is still your responsibility. It looks very different every year. Discipline is still necessary. She needs you to help her to maintain her compass.

Further, she will need your wisdom because trouble is looking for her. She needs a 'heads-up' about what is waiting for her in the world. You do this better than anyone else! Do not assume that someone else has it.

**WORK ETHIC.**

She needs your work ethic. Work ethic and pride in her work will be important. She cannot be successful and be lazy. She needs to be assisted with developing the best work ethic. You need to be her example—her first and most dependable model for awesome work ethic.

She needs to get to work, church, and other places on time, do her best job and give her best effort everywhere she exists, and finally, be a contributor wherever she is. You need to model and demonstrate excellence so that she is required to do the same.

This is not a 'do as I say, not as I do' generation. If you lack a work ethic, then you cannot expect her to do anything differently.

Her work ethic develops her work reputation; her overall reputation as a dependable person.

## TRUTH.

Many men struggle with the truth. You cannot afford to lie to her or allow her to bear witness to your lying or pay for your lies. Your lies cost her; they cost her something. Teach her how to be truthful.

She needs to know the truth. The information she has is what she uses to make decisions. If she has faulty information, then she will make some bad decisions.

If you lie to her, then so can others. Please do not expect others to treat her better than you do. If you lie, so will she. It is what you taught her. She needs to tell the truth and live in truth.

Are you going to be angry when her mate lies to her? Is that okay? If not, then PLEASE STOP LYING!

## EDUCATE.

Do you value education? How much value do you place on it? How much education do you have? That's the level she will achieve unless you persuade her to do more. You need to exert your influence over her to inspire her to achieve at the level you have dreamed of for her. What do you want her to achieve? Does she know that? Was she receptive to your desire for her?

Is she motivated intrinsically or extrinsically? What are you doing to assist her with her motivation? What are you going to do when she needs to be motivated? Do you know what motivates your daughter?

Education changes her opportunities and her confidence. She needs all of the possible tools so that she can have all the possible ways to be successful. You need to ensure that she is supported in her educational endeavors. Like, dad, she will need your guidance and emotional support during this journey.

If you are short of your personal educational goals, then return to school so that you can reach your goals. This is also lifting your spirit. When your spirit is lifted, you can be a better dad.

Show her how to splurge with excellence. You go first.

**TIME.**

She spells love TIME. All that she wants is your time. She wants what you cannot make and what she does not control: Your Time. Money is good; Time is best.

When she asks for your time, make it happen. Excuses are unacceptable!

There's a father who did not know his daughter for many years. Then once she knew about him, he went to prison, so their first face-to-face encounter was under supervision. When he was released, she anticipated the promises he made to her would be fulfilled. But not quite the way he promised or what she imagined because they do not spend time together. She asks. He makes excuses. He makes empty promises. She reduces him in her life each time. She no longer respects him as a father. She does not take his opinion into account for major decisions. He has no voice in her life.

She just wants his time—the time she deserves. She is not unique. She is not asking for anything special. She wants what is rightfully hers—your time.

Let it be your idea. Schedule an appointment for her. Just like your golf tee time and your haircut, she needs a time that belongs to her—by herself. During this time, you spend with her, you are exercising your influence and voice in her life. Without this time, your voice competes with Google, and her friends. You usually will be challenged, and you will likely lose the battle.

Take time to teach, explain, emphasize, grow, share, and equip. When she makes a mistake and you haven't taught her that concept, it is your fault. Time is critical. She needs it. Her success depends on it.

**TENDERNESS.**

Remember that she is your daughter, your seed, so you need to be tender. You need to be tender toward her. You are her measure of how a man will treat her. If you are rough, then she expects rough. Chances are you will not approve but as you reflect on your actions toward her, consider that she saw it with you first.

Be tender. Be firm. Be understanding. Be tender.

**MORE. MORE.**

Dad, do more. 'I already do it all.' Do you both agree with that statement? Have you ever considered asking her what she needs more of from you? You may be surprised by her response.

Do more. Do something different. Develop what you will share with her every day or week.

She needs more. She deserves more.

## GOD.

Make sure that she knows God. Do you know God? Does she see you attend church? Does she attend church with you? Does she understand the importance of a relationship with God? Does she have her own relationship with God? Did you share God with her?

Do you talk about what God has done for you?

## WORSHIP.

Do you have a relationship with God? Does she know your relationship with God? Does she have a relationship with God? Do you nourish her relationship with God?

Her relationship and her worship are necessary and are also your responsibility. She must have this relationship with God. You need to ensure that it is cemented and cannot be moved by outside influences. Can you imagine your daughter telling you that she converted to some other faith because you left her vulnerable to assumption? Pray to see how she needs you to share with her. Pray for her daily. Sending scriptures daily also helps.

## PRAY.

Prayer—is the most powerful conversation in the world. Do you pray? Do you pray consistently? Do you pray for her? Does she hear you pray for her? Do you pray with her? Does she pray? Does she know how to pray?

Your prayers have power and influence over her life. You need to pray for her daily. You need to pray for her in her presence. You can influence her prayer life by a consistent one of your own. Keep her before the Lord—she needs it. She needs your prayers.

The enemy is counting on you neglecting prayer because of the vulnerability it causes you to be in front of her. But quite the opposite will result. She will see your heart. She will see a different you than she ever knew. She will be transformed too.

Pray.

Without ceasing.

Without excuse.

Without hesitation.

## STUDY.

'I don't like to read.' This is not school; this is God's word. Read it. Meditate on it. Memorize it. Share it. Study it.

Help her to understand what God's word says and how to apply it to her life.

When you don't understand, get some help. Ask another man at your church.

Study how to show thyself approved. You are God's workmanship.

**FAST.**

Yes, fast and pray for the spiritual upliftment of your family, especially your daughter. Give up food or social media or something else as a demonstration of sacrifice to God and submission to Him.

Fast for God-sized results.

---

That sums up your job description. It seems like your name should be longer based on these descriptions but you are stuck with DAD. Make her proud to call you DAD.

**LENGTH OF PARENTING.**

You are designed to parent her whole life and yours. This may seem strange but while you may change how you parent, you still parent. There's no vacation, time off, or breaks. Your parenting just looks different as she grows and grows up.

She still needs your wisdom, guidance, and advice. She still needs and wants your protection and provision.

You are still daddy and no one can take your place or try to substitute for your job unless you allow it due to absenteeism.

**TRADITION: ABANDON vs. RETAINING.**

An average of the two results in above-average results.

When people say, 'I am old school,' I laugh. Either we already know that based on your behavior or you don't know what you just said because neither your words nor deeds match the meaning of those words. I believe in modernity, except when parenting is in the conversation.

Parenting is challenging; your parents will challenge you first about your parenting techniques used with their granddaughter. Gently remind them of how they raised you and you will establish some support. Remind them to frame it that way and those challenges will subside.

As for the rest of the world, take a deep breath and remind yourself that she belongs to you—she has your DNA and wears your name. She is your report card—do not be swayed by outsiders.

When you were 12, you promised that when you were a dad, you would not do the same things that your parents did. Since being 12 years old, your perspective has broadened exponentially—so much so that you regret ever saying that because now you know why your parents did much of what they did, you are grateful for their strict curfews, academic accountability, in your business regarding friends and destinations. You have shared this with them, or at least you should have by now.

Take a look at yourself. Could your parents have done anything differently to make you a better person? Could you have done anything differently to be a better child than a better person? Based on who you are today, do you regret the parents and the parenting that you were given?

My commitment, and maybe yours as well, is to be a better parent than what I had to produce a better child, consequently, a better adult, than I am.

Because of that commitment, there will be some traditional values attached to your 'modern' parenting.

We are after the best possible woman for the rest of her life. She needs you to be firm. She needs your consistent presence and counsel and guidance.

'Modern' is because you compete for your daughter with the outside world which comes directly into your home via the palm of her hand: the internet, and her friends, who know as little as she does. That phone is your security and your worst enemy. You have to get ahead of that issue—first and foremost. Do not let the internet guide your child; regret will be imminent.

So tradition had to intervene in modern, reminding her of the standards and rules and expectations you have taught her to live her life by. Once you establish those standards, expectations, and rules have to hold up to those same standards, expectations, and rules. She will use those standards, expectations, and rules to govern the people in her life—friends as well as future mates.

This is invaluable for your investment and influences your ability to parent. You will have to determine what those are but I know that some long-standing rules at my house are:

(1) no hats worn inside the house,

(2) check your car before you get on the road for long distances,

(3) home by curfew,

(4) keep a certain amount of cash on your person,

(5) get good grades, and,

(6) consult the parent when making new decisions.

So, remember whether traditional or not, you are still her parent. Teaching is not optional. You want your voice to stand out in her head when you are not available, and she can recall what would my dad do or say. You want her to recall your words, your voice, and your experience—all of which you have shared. You only have one chance to get this correct. What will you teach her? What will she remember? What will she do with your teaching?

Don't be afraid to parent your daughter. You will not regret it.

The Power of the Daddy/Daughter Relationship

My Dearest KTK:

    I have watched you grow and often wondered how time slipped by so fast. I adjust my eyes and see you anew for even your " youth has passed". It seemed like only yesterday that your innocent voice called my name, now it whispers a child's sweet name and a " Hubby " has entered the game. Sometimes I miss the times we shared as selfish as that might be, but I let you go to find your place to be that "Dove" set free!

    I know it was not easy when I questioned the choices you made, but God had set a "standard" and I was "charged" to make the grade. The water in your eyes hid the real words you wanted to say, somehow you regained your composure and kindly tucked them away. Sometimes I did not get it right but in all, I meant no harm, I wanted to see you get it right and share with the world your charm.  It takes a lot to raise a girl, and daughters are the best, I pray for you as you journey through to succeed in every test!

    The sparkle in your eyes tells me all will be okay, you were not afraid to leave me and meet the challenges of the day.  Daddys are overprotective, like a lion that guards its pride, we show, we teach, and cry sometimes but we take it all in stride. Even in your failures, I would not let them get you down, I offered you words of encouragement to help turn those things around.

    I feel elated and I know you are going to make it. You have a family of your own and nothing on this earth will shake it. When your children look at you, with the same eyes you looked at me, know that they are a reflection of how you used to be. They may not always get it right and will find ways to make you "Mad", but keep in mind and never forget that this is the greatest gift you ever had! So cherish them as you watch them grow as I have done with you, for a successful life is ahead of them but you will have to help them through!!!  That's just what mommies and daddies do!

May love always cover you and may the Spirit of forgiveness always rest within you. I love each of each you my special " KTK"...Kathy, Tiffany, and Krystal.

Dad!

*In Your Hands*

## HER JOB AS A DAUGHTER

The daughter is the little girl that you dreamed of and asked for because of your reasons. She is your princess. You would do ANYTHING for her.

**WANTED: GREAT DAUGHTER**

Good grades

Great attitude

Keep your room clean

Dream BIG dreams

Communicator

Respectful

Loving

Caring

Listens

Obedient

Admired

**HOW DO YOU GET THE GRAT DAUGHTER?**

A great daughter requires a father who does some work.

Father, you have to work and communicate and teach.

You have to teach her what she needs to know. You have to teach her what she needs to survive and succeed in the real world.

Most Dads do not have a problem teaching. The real issue is the assumptions and the metaphorical language. Your investment makes her great. Are you asking yourself that if you don't invest will she not be great? She can be great without you but she will have to depend on people to whom she will owe her knowledge and experience, which means she may have to sacrifice herself at some point. Do you want that for her? No, you don't.

There are not many dads who claim that they are perfect or even great, but their daughters will reveal lots about your presence or absence. Greatness starts with you—be there!

## WANT AD: A GREAT DAUGHTER!

A great daughter!

A great listener!

Obedient.

Kind.

Loving.

Equipped to learn.

*In Your Hands*

## DESCRIPTION OF GREAT DAUGHTER

Nothing is perfect about a daughter. As a daughter, I am not perfect, however to my father, I am perfect. In his eyes, the world should treat me as perfect.

A great daughter tries to do all things that represent you well. We need to obey, respect, learn, grow, and trust.

Daughters, and women, learn differently so we need to be taught differently. That is a vague concept. The father does not know that the lesson was not effective until she does something 'wrong,' which he has to correct.

Great daughters are honest. With herself and others.

Great daughters make their dads proud and when they disappoint their dads, they apologize.

Great daughters seek wisdom, from Dad and approved others.

She also seeks his approval, sometimes it is implied, rather than obvious. This is a point of contention, but communication clears up the matter.

She must be a great communicator as well. This is one of those who do as he says, not as he does. A great daughter understands that she needs to be a great communicator, but her father may not be a great communicator.

A great daughter understands the culture of her family so that she knows that her behavior and decisions impact her father, and he has to fix any mistakes that she makes.

A great daughter keeps her word and understands the value of her words. She needs to understand her influence over others.

A great daughter loves without condition. She is equipped to love without limits. She knows the risk and takes it anyway. She learned from her father. A great daughter is compassionate to others. She is also forgiving.

She is responsible for her finances and tries to give to others when she is able.

A great daughter listens and is proactive about goals and life.

A great daughter has character. She is an upstanding citizen. She is conscientious about her dealings with people. She respects herself, others, and the environment. She contributes to and enhances her community.

She is educated. She reads. She researches. She is inquisitive.

## YOUR METAPHORS vs. HER KNOWLEDGE.

When do you consider what your daughter should know versus what she knows, how much work do you need to do? Her knowledge is your responsibility.

Her knowledge affects your relationship. As a daughter, I am my father's report card. Did he do his job? This ranges from changing a tire to managing money to managing relationships. At the end of every day, your grade is based on is she equipped as the girl who will be a woman, without your consent and despite your procrastination and protest.

If you made a list of what she needs to know—tangible and intangible, what would that include? How did you develop that list?

If you died tomorrow, what will she need to learn alone? That is not ideal, but we need to place a perspective on the level of urgency, and importance, and stop the 'I have time' thought process.

*In Your Hands*

My father was a metaphor and he used metaphors often. I had to interpret data and information, read between the lines and think my way out of his metaphorical maze of messages—all before Google.

When I say metaphors, I will also extend that to 'man speak' and 'man code.' This means that you are speaking in a special language that only you understand. She will have to decide what you mean, what you want her to do, and what she did wrong.

I am suggesting that you are giving her too much to decipher. I am hoping that you will tell her exactly what she needs to know, what she needs to do, and then you need to teach her how to understand and survive metaphors. Sometimes, we believe that we have taught our children what we mean or the back story of our processes and the resulting actions, but in reality, we have not. If you are not leading explanations with words such as 'the reason for this is' or 'I do this in this manner because,' then you are hoping that she is catching what she is observing. That is not measurable until she does or does not make the decision that you approve of. That is not timely though. The amount of damage is too much, too late.

Best practice: teach those metaphors, and define the terms that you are going to use so that she can be defined as mutually successful. Teach her!

## HER UNDERSTANDING OF YOUR TEACHING, METAPHORICAL CONVERSATION, AND UNSPOKEN TRADITIONS/STANDARDS/RULES.

You have some unspoken rules, and unstated standards, which you need to share with her authentically. She needs your expectations so that she can be successful.

My father wants to be sure that I mature into a great woman so he taught me how to drive several different types of vehicles: a pick-up truck, a dump truck, an 18-wheeler, and two types of tractors. He never stated why this was important. I could only assume that he wanted me to know how to drive any vehicle so that if I were ever in a less than secure situation I could drive any vehicle and get myself to safety. But I did not know to ask that question and he never stated his reasons. This makes him a great dad but I still had to interpret some information.

If you speak about the matter directly, then it does not minimize the value of the lesson. Tell her directly. Teach her the questions that she needs to ask to get the answers that she wants.

Tell her the rules, the standards, and the traditions of you and your family. Teach them to her and then watch you and her be successful. This is one of the most important parts of your job. She needs to hear your voice in her head when she is making a decision and it is strong enough so that that your voice is not overridden by the voice of another, like her mate, her friends, or Google.

*In Your Hands*

# COMMUNICATION
—What this means.

Communication is the exchange of information between two or more people. Communication between you and your daughter is verbal, non—verbal, body language, and even, mental. Your communication is learned and taught, experienced and cultivated.

Communication with your daughter needs to be intentional. You need to plan to talk and communicate with your daughter. You need to schedule time through events, and occasions, so that you will have dedicated time to communicate with your daughter about what she needs to know. This is also time for you to learn and attempt to understand her. Intentional means planned, scheduled, and dedicated.

Saturday mornings were my time with my father. This was time well spent when I learned all of the things that I needed to know and say, all of what I needed to learn and see. We had other moments as well but this was our dedicated time. We spent Sunday watching football together as well.

Communication needs to be safe so that she continues to talk to you and depend on your instruction and tutelage. Safe means that you listen and you teach and advise her on her decisions and directions. She needs to be able to tell you things that will bring you to your knees, which may be both internally and externally. She needs to be able to share that information with you—directly and immediately.

There was an occasion when I needed to tell my father some life-changing information. He was there. He listened. He held me when I cried. He did not judge me. Then he handled it for me. Afterward, he taught me some valuable lessons. I listened. He affirmed me. He was my confidant; my safe place. Not my friend. My Father.

You as the safe place means that she opts for you rather than the internet or her equally as her knowledge-lacking friends. The safe place brings the security she needs. She needs the security that you should provide. Her information is secure and private with you. You are her advisor and her secret keeper. In some instances, all of her friends may seek your advice as to their safe place as well. Our daughters need a SAFE place.

Direct and non-metaphorical communication, as mentioned in the previous chapter, is required for a successful woman to be the outcome. The metaphors will also be taught as you spend more time and teach. You should be receptive to questions and you answer those questions. You have to share your innermost thoughts, fears, and concerns with her so that you can offer her the opportunity to do the same.

Your communication is her air: her oxygen. Oxygen gives life to the rest of the body. She needs your communication. You need to be open. She depends on you to decipher the garbage that she will see, hear, and possibly ingest. You need to tell her the secrets to success with her career, her other parent, her mother, her mate, her life, her friends, and her children, future of course. There is so much information and strategy to navigate and you naturally want to minimize her mistakes and her margin of error, while maximizing her knowledge, wisdom, and intuition.

You will have to ensure that she embodies your definition of common sense as well. The world does not teach that—you do! Intuition does not come to an unprepared mind. You have to prepare her mind to have the type of intuition that translates into great decision-making that you will be proud of.

Your creative communication is required. Use every aspect: text messaging, email, social media, video chat, mail (Yes! US Mail.), and the phone.

Text messages are a great tool. A text can be sent any time of day and contain anything—a message, a photo, a song, or a link. Send her an affirmation daily. Send a regular 'I love you.' Send a random 'I am thinking about you.'

Email her a letter. Send information to her which directs her thoughts, and provide instructions and information regularly (every week or two). Email her a video and directions on how to change a tire, scholarship applications, and even your vacation list or college list. She then has this as a reference for later. Send recipes, safety tips, news stories, and anything else you need her to know.

Social media may be a stretch for you and may challenge you at all levels, however, you need to stretch so that you can meet at her level, such that she can see your care and your reach. Social media helps you to understand her thought process, which leads to being able to share with her ways to redirect her thought process.

Video chat so that you can see her when you cannot get in front of her in the flesh. Do it regularly.

Mail! Yes, mail it in the mailbox so that she can open it and read your handwriting. You may have never written a note to her so you need to write some things for her so that she has some keepsakes of you. Mail her packages—surprise care packages—with things that she likes. Do you know what she likes? Snacks? Body wash fragrances? Perfumes? Shoe brands and shoe size? Shirt size? Favorite color? Remind her that she is important to you.

The phone is the easiest form of communication. Pick up the phone and call. Talk about anything. Ask questions. Make her think. Get her attention. Keep her thinking. Keep her talking. She needs to recognize your voice.

Be creative in all that you do. You are modeling what she will later repeat. You are building a woman who needs to be nurturing, caring, loving, fierce, faithful, loyal, resilient, a warrior, and sometimes a weapon of mass destruction. For all of those roles, she needs your guidance and leadership.

Communication needs to be mutual. As you communicate, she learns to and she becomes comfortable and judicious in doing so. This also includes being able to understand the timing of certain conversations. She needs mutual and equitable communication. She also has to be your safe place.

You need to be honest as you engage in this communication. She needs your honesty so that she knows how to do the same. Again, honesty is taught through observation and demonstration. She needs to see you be honest in your communication and your activities. She needs to be an honest woman. Someone will be her mate and she needs to be able, to be honest. Help her to be honest by being honest with her. You are the explanation for so many of her questions and her background.

Truth and honesty need to lead to trust and trustworthiness. She needs you to be trustworthy. She needs to be able to trust you. She needs to be able to trust herself. This trust enables other things to be possible.

Trustworthiness becomes a necessity as she grows from birth to adulthood. For her to be trustworthy, she has to learn that from you and she will need to do that with you. She needs also to recognize when someone is not trustworthy. More importantly, she needs to know how to discern and determine that they are not trustworthy and what that means; then she needs to manage that lack of trustworthiness if that does happen. How will she break away from such situations? Without your instruction, guidance, and wisdom?

Share with her the type of commodity trustworthiness is. She needs to understand what happens if she lets that trustworthiness be sacrificed. How will that trust be earned again? If she knows its importance then she will protect it better.

Communicate about communication and its importance. Empower her to be transparent in her communication with a love that leaves others emotionally stable. And with some dignity.

Communication will be her key to success in all the areas of her life. You are the lead teacher on this matter.

She is counting on you to invest in her at a very high level, so don't fail us.

*In Your Hands*

# MENTAL LANDMINES

Landmines are sections of land which are outfitted with bombs to provide security for the property beyond the landmine. The two types are anti-personnel and anti-vehicle. The anti-personnel is designed to explode with as little pressure as four (4) pounds applied to the area. This means that once you place your foot on the area which has a bomb underneath will blow up as you put your full weight down in transition while you are walking. So, while you are in mid-stride, you will blow up.

You are designed to teach her where the mental landmines are. You have them and so do her mother and her future mate. She will develop them as well. She needs to know how to recognize and manage herself and others to be successful.

She needs to understand what the landmines are. She needs to know what the thought of others, as well as the health and well—being of others, will impact her mental stability, health, and well—being.

These mental and emotional landmines will also be metaphorical. She needs to understand that these are metaphorical for the unspoken rules of different people who are important to her and who she will meet.

How will you teach her to discern the presence of the landmines? How will you show her to discern the magnitude of the landmine? How large? How many unspoken rules and issues exist? How will she survive the unspoken standard and rules once she discovers them if they cannot be dismantled?

These landmines also include other types of baggage and underlying agendas. Help her to understand, discern, to disarm, and survive the mental and emotional landmines.

Where you wrong as a dad is that you expect her to figure it out alone. She cannot do that without great instruction. If she does not have great and thorough instruction, then she will be damaged—some of which are irreparable, and costly.

We cannot afford mistakes that could have been avoided.

Do not let her guess what you expect from her and what you want her to know, how you expect her to treat herself, and how she should communicate with others.

## HER INTEGRITY

As we define integrity, it starts with the truth, then adds to that truth, a behavior that is driven by moral and ethical principles.

Her integrity establishes her character with others. She will be judged by her integrity or lack thereof. You will always want her to be seen in the best image, with people having the best opinion of her.

She will use your behavior to determine her behavior. Are you an example of integrity? She uses your behavior to determine her own, so what will she see is what will she do.

Will you be proud of that which she repeats? Will you be proud of her reputation if she does everything that you do?

Help her to shape her integrity. Help her with the practice of integrity. She needs to practice making the right decisions. Sometimes the right choice is harder than the easy choice, which could lead down the wrong path; which sometimes lasts indefinitely.

Be intentional.

# AVOID the METAPHORICAL LIFESTYLE MISTAKE

Many men speak in metaphors. It comes easy to you. You have mastered this over the years and as you navigated life, you have become good at it. However, she is not good at it. She does not understand you. She does not want you to know that she does not understand what you are saying because she wants to impress you.

Start explaining your statements and share the meaning behind your words.

**HER LIFE'S PHILOSOPHY**

Philosophy is defined as a system of principles for guidance in practical affairs.

The philosophy of life is defined as any philosophical view or vision of the nature or purpose of life or of the way that life should be lived.

She will also develop that philosophy based on what she sees and what she knows and what you share. As you develop her life's philosophy, consider what she already knows: your life's philosophy.

What is it? Can you put it in writing? Does she understand each component? Does she share your attitude and ideals?

Integrity. Honest. Family. Respect. Work Ethic. These are some of the elements of the life philosophy which she should espouse. This is what she will be known for, valued, and respected. It is the code by which she will live.

You have shaped this for her entire life. By the time, she is an adult, you need to make sure that all of those details are finalized and perfected.

The Power of the Daddy/Daughter Relationship

This is essential to her foundation as a woman. She will accomplish great things with a sound foundation. This foundation is paired with a great background so that she can propel herself toward all of those goals.

Her life's philosophy is your report card—it is the culmination of all things which you have worked hard to instill within her.

What words do you want to describe her? Which of these will be used to describe her?

| Insightful | Distinctive | Beautiful |
|---|---|---|
| Courageous | Thoughtful | Spiritual |
| Respectable | Profound | Concise |
| Respected | Provocative | Conspicuous |
| Admired | Educated | Leader |
| Amazing | Considerate | Facilitator |
| Integrity | Caring | Thought-provoking |
| Wonderful | Work—ethic | Kind |
| Loving | Conscientious | Motivating |
| Compassionate | Inspiring | Charismatic |
| Powerful | Tender | Helpful |
| Curious | Trustworthy | Philanthropist |
| Classy | Intelligent | Perceptive |

This requires your undivided attention—to shape her life's philosophy. Help her to write down her philosophy, along with mission and vision statements.

It is what directs her path. It is what drives her decisions.

## HER DECISION—MAKING and PROCESS

Whew! Every dad's concern is 'will she make the right choices.' That is a valid concern. Her mistakes ultimately cost you, both financially and time, worry, and some sleepless nights. Her sound decision—making is the only way that you will rest. How will she make decisions? Will it be a list? A note? A conversation with you?

How will she make decisions in such a manner where she is either successful or learning? Your encouragement and feedback weigh a ton. She needs your heavy reassurance or your gentle redirection.

The real question is what do you do when she makes an error? How do you fix the situation? How do you leave her self—esteem and dignity intact? How do you support her so that her pride in this mistake does not overtake her into a bad space?

You are charged with ensuring that her mistakes don't break her.

I remember one of the best times between my father and me was when I had a life-changing event: I was pregnant. I had missed school to be examined and scheduled an appointment for an abortion. My mother found out about my missing school. She kicked me out of the house and dropped me off at my dad's house because I would not tell her what happened and why I missed school. Within a few minutes of being at my dad's, I shared the entire situation. I cried. He pulled me into his arms. He reassured me that everything was going to be okay. He then did only what my father could do: he handled it.

He made sure that what happened did not break me. These decisions are not easy. They are extremely hard. Among those same difficult decisions are marriage, college, car buying, house purchase, and other life-changing decisions.

These are big decisions that leave a wake of consequences or good favor.

She will face many decisions in her life as you know. Some of them will have great outcomes and others will be a complete disaster. No matter what the decision or the outcome, she needs your reassurance and support—through it all.

You cannot keep her from falling, making mistakes, or even failing, but you can keep her from remaining in that place, no matter how dark it may be.

## LISTEN

Listen.

Listen.

Wait.

Listen.

Listen.

Listen.

Listen until she stops talking.


She is going to talk but not as much as if she does not think you are listening. So listen with your eyes, your ears, your hands, your head, your heart, your feet, your focus, your intentions, and your closed mouth.

Listen with your body language. Sit completely still—focusing completely on what she is saying. Listen with your mouth closed. Don't talk. Don't interrupt while she is talking. Don't try to solve the problem which she has not presented. When she is done talking, then asks 'do you want me to help you with that matter, or did you just want me to know.' Action versus information: what do you need me to do? Let her start with that so that you will know which direction to go with the next step(s).

Listening with your complete focus on her is the best thing for her. She needs to be able to have you as an audience.

You have competition for her attention. Because she is talking to you means that she respects you and values your voice, which includes your advice, your opinion, and even your judgment. You as a parent compete for her ear. The internet, her friends, her enemies, and everything else impacts the weight of your message and the weight of your influence, and whether your voice is on mute or not.

As her audience, you are powerful, influential, and a game-changer. You are her first man love. She is going to compare every mate in her life to you. You will be the standard for what she defines as an acceptable mate.

Listening is essential to understanding who she is, what she likes, what she thinks, what she feels, and how she processes information.

Further, while you are listening, she is learning to listen, an essential skill, for a successful life. Learning to listen is hard for some people. Help her to learn to listen with an understanding of the other person's needs and concerns, fears, and questions.

Listen. Don't rush. Don't interrupt.

Once you hear her, and she answers the question of action or information, then help her with the concerns that she shared. Teach her how to problem solve. She needs to understand your thought process and your logic so that you can help her to develop her own.

But the most important part is to listen at a level where she feels important and respected so that she keeps talking.

## HER EXAMPLE—HER ROLE MODEL

Do as I say, not as I do?

Do as I do, not as I say.

You should reconsider the parenting mantra of 'do as I say, not as I do.' Do what I say and disregard what I do. Do not watch me—only hear me. That is not a great plan.

My son asked to throw something out of the window and his father said no. My son's response was 'But Dad you did it.' For so many reasons, this was interesting and everybody learned something that day.

When my son, who was 3 years old, shared with me that he was upset that he could not do what he saw done and it seemed exciting to do, I was amazed. He was 3 years old. He thinks that he can do what he sees being done and he should be able to do so.

What if he had just rolled down the window and threw out the item? What happens next makes all of the difference in how this day concludes. The result is probably some level of discipline, and while quite appropriate, is extremely wrong. The fault belongs to the dad. He did something wrong and was teaching others to do the same.

Have you ever done that—taught your daughter something that you later paid for and had to unteach? Have you ever taught something that you did not know that she was watching and had learned? My son's father did not realize that he had done it.

Father's lesson: don't do anything that you do not want them to do.

I hear your debate: 'but I am the adult.' You are right, you are the adult. You can do whatever you want. You will need to recall that there are consequences for all of those actions, some of them are more costly than others. Can you afford for your daughter to experience those negative consequences? What will you have to pay as a result of the consequence of poorly and inadvertently taught lessons?

When you consider all that you have taught her, what do you need to reteach to correct the wrong learnings? This is something that you may need to reevaluate from time to time. You will need to show her the correct way to do things then if you want to show her the shortcut, then do so, but more importantly, tell her the why.

Men do tend to not share the why or the logic behind a decision or the technique used. Women need that explanation to trust and accept that transformation as offered. If you don't want her to modify the process, then tell her. Otherwise, when she does modify it, you will not be able to change that.

This is a great time to insert that you treat your daughter differently than your son. Listen to her when she explains why she feels that way. Evaluate your actions to make she that if you do allow your son to do what you won't allow your daughter to do, at least you own it. Please be sure you are honest about it. Then explain to her why. Then stick to it.

The double standards exist for a reason. She needs to know your protection and its value for her life, her self—esteem, and her reputation. It is hard to support and defend and condone, but it is necessary.

Evaluate your actions to make sure that what she is observing and learning is what you want her to see and learn. You are her role model. You are her hero. You are her standard of the future man in her life. You are her Father. Her Daddy. The man in her life. She needs to be able to trust you. She needs to be able to rely on you. She needs to be able to depend on you. She needs to be able to look at you and recall what she needs to do.

You are her role model. Take your role seriously. She depends on you.

## The Power of the Daddy/Daughter Relationship

### To Rachel by Aaron Dallas

A father rarely fully releases parental control; eases the reigns, maybe! I have watched closely my daughter grow from infancy to a responsible young lady. While our daughter matriculated through high school, I tried to be nonchalant about planting good Christian mentors in her life. Other than parents, who do you trust with guidance and development over your child? Thankfully, I really didn't have to look far from TCWW. Many opportunities existed at TCWW to grow and nurture my daughter and to help us both understand the value of an actively engaged father.

I desired to put the right ingredients in my daughter's life to help mature her along the way. I can identify this best in what we enjoy doing together: gardening. When we garden we have an open dialogue to identify a certain result we want to achieve through gardening. We select our soil, item to plant, ready the soil, place the seeds, and nurture the seeds to ensure the outcome we have discussed. We visualize the finished product to know where to begin.

This is my approach to parenting my daughter. Even now with her in college, she knows that I am here for her. In raising her, for me, the finished product is an adult who is capable of coping in the real world. She may not have all the answers or abilities, but she knows I have planted seeds in her spirit that will help her succeed in her endeavors. Her growth in life will continue to develop through the struggles of being away from home; and because of the seeds growing deep within the soil of her soul, she has an authentic path to follow. She will have that potential to manage whatever comes her way because I as her father took the time to show her how.

The first question for me as a father to answer is 'How do you mature without imposing'? Well, three things hold true:

1. I pray about what I intend to communicate
2. I listen intently, and
3. I sit closely

I am mindful to be there when she has to reach out to me. My goal is to allow her to sense and know that what we are communicating about is as important to me, as it is to her. As a father, I must admit there are times when it is difficult to just stop tending to the soul of the soil you have been nurturing for 19-years. You can never take your eye off its growth or you'll miss an opportunity to keep the sprinklers of wisdom showing it with love, care, and wisdom. One such instance is the "D" word. DATING!

The bible says in Proverbs 23:6 "train a child in the way they should go, and when they are old they will not part from it." As my daughter got older and boys took an interest in her, I made it a priority to take her on her first date. And, from that day on we concocted a phrase called "Daddy daughter Day". At times we would just go out and enjoy a movie and ice cream, or a walk in the neighborhood. It is up to me to have set the example on how to interact while on a date. The boundaries to select and maintain. The way she is to carry herself. So, when the conversation came up regarding actually going on a physical date I had to remind myself what I'd planted in my family garden. I planted on good soil, and so I am to trust her decisions as a college student. I trust that my training was intentional, on purpose, and with total dependency on Jesus the perfect gardener. The key to fatherhood is to trust our heavenly Father!

Aaron Dallas

## QUESTIONS

She will ask so many—ALL OF THEM.

The purpose of the questions is for her to understand what she needs to know and how you think about things.

She needs to be able to ask questions. Nurture her inquisitive nature. Help her to develop a logical and healthy mindset and thought process.

Every girl would benefit from the cool, calm, and collected demeanor of a man who could share insight into important strategy and other details that makes the difference between a daughter who becomes a great networker, negotiator, and nurturer.

When a girl—turned—woman becomes a strategist and a successful businesswoman, you can give yourself credit for making sure that she had the necessary for that success.

These questions may cause you to laugh, cry, and thoughtfully consider your own life. She may annoy, anger, antagonize, frustrate, and upset you because she questions you, your decisions, your strategies, your techniques, and your mind.

She will ask questions at just the wrong time, in the wrong environment, on the wrong occasion, for the wrong reasons, and about the most difficult topics when you least expect it.

Some of her questions may hurt, and the rest of them will cause you to consider your position in life.

She may cause you to reconsider your thought process and your decisions. She will ask you and challenge you—she will create strength, doubt, and promise.

She needs access to information, which you possess and need to be able to willingly release, hence the questions.

She has a billion questions. She needs to be able to ask you. She needs you to receive those questions with a great disposition.

Questions that I asked my Dad and some you should anticipate:

1. Who am I?
2. Who are you?
3. Why do you do what you do?
4. What do you think I should do?
5. What do you mean?
6. Can you repeat that?
7. Can you explain . . . again?
8. Do you love me?
9. Do you love my mom?
10. How will I know that another person loves me?
11. How did you know when you loved someone else?

These are enough to give you an idea about where this could go, so you need to prepare to hear her questions.

- Answer them all honestly, regardless of the perceived outcome.
- Answer the ones that you don't want because she asked and the truth and your forthrightness are important to her
- Answer the questions that she won't ask because she needs that information because she needs to grow from that knowledge
- Share the truth with her about everything
- De—mystify yourself so that she can connect with you
- Especially those questions about her mother and any family history

# ANSWERS

Where there are questions, then answers should follow.

She was just asking, but she needs you to answer her.

You compete with everyone for her to answer her questions.

It is you versus Google. You versus her friends and her frenemies. You versus society.

It is you versus anybody who will talk to her. To answer your questions, you have to be available. You have to be present. You have to be available. You need to be 'in the room.' Your time with her is critical.

When she asks, you need to hear her, make time to hear her, and be here for her.

You only have a finite period where your voice drowns out others, where your opinion is not in competition with others, and when you are viewed as the subject matter expert rather than the 'trust but verify' attitude.

This is your time to be the Father—Leader—Expert—Hero—Champion.

Answer her questions with truth in love with love. Tell her the truth. The truth may hurt and she needs that so that she does not commit the sins that you committed and does not repeat the error of your ways. Most importantly, you will help correct those new potential errors which await her—the new issue and the unforeseen situations that could occur.

There is a list in your head of things that she cannot do that she does not even know about. Further, she needs answers to questions that she does not know that she has yet. You need to answer questions that she may never ask and ones that she does not know to ask.

Answer the questions. All of them. Honestly. With explanations. Without metaphors. Don't lose your voice to anyone or anything or the internet.

Tell her what she needs to know.

Be prepared to repeat yourself.

*In Your Hands*

# THE LEANING TOWER OF PISA

## THE CURRENT STATUS OF HER WELL—BEING AND YOUR RELATIONSHIP

In Pisa, Italy, there's a structure, a freestanding bell tower that because of an unstable foundation, leans 4 degrees. Pisa means marshland. The tower was built on unstable ground. Not sure that the builder knows that the tower would eventually lean.

If the builder knew that it would lean, then why did they build it anyway?

Why do people intentionally visit such a 'spectacle'? They have found value in something with obvious imperfections. If it had not been leaning, would it have been as popular? Probably not.

Now, consider your daughter. Is her foundation stable? Will she be leaning? Will she be popular because of her imperfections?

How do you manage her instability and status? What can you do as a father? Do you review her phone messages and activity (this of course won't work if she is over 18)?

Again, regular conversations help this situation. Your voice is influential. You should use it to keep her whole.

The status of your relationship—what is it? How would you grade your relationship? How would she grade your relationship?

What we both know for sure is that you need it not to lean any further. If it is leaning further than 5 (five) degrees, then you need to start to stabilize the foundation.

How can you do that?

- Regular conversations
- Daily text messages
- Weekly date nights
- Monthly events
- Birthday dinner/event alone
- Topic to achieve each year—what will you teach her this year or until she learns how to do it at the expert level

These are ideas that will guarantee your more stable foundation and a better relationship. She needs to hear your voice. She needs to hear your voice in her head when someone tries to tell her something contrary.

She needs that stable foundation. She is growing up in an unstable world with unstable people and this instability keeps changing. She needs you.

The other lesson that she needs to learn from you is conflict resolution. The ability to save a relationship and solve the conflict in that same relationship is different between men and women. She needs to be able to resolve issues and still maintain the relationship. Women do not do this well. We hold grudges and do not forgive and we treat it like it's personal all of the time. Don't get too excited about that confession. I am trying to help the next generations.

We need a course on how to make that transition—value and retain the relationship while disagreeing, being disagreeable, and surviving that disagreement.

Tip that tower back into the stable and upright position.

## YOUR VISION OF HER

### PUT EVERYTHING ON THE TABLE—TRANSPARENCY
### PUT EVERYTHING ON THE LINE—RISK

Transparency.

You have a dream, vision, and goals for her. You have had this since she was born. What is it? Tell her. Why doesn't she know it already? What happens if she does not want to follow your plan for her?

Tell her what you think about, what you dream about, what you consider important, what is negotiable, and what is not negotiable.

These are details and facts that she needs to know so when she does something that does not meet your approval and you are utterly disappointed, then she is not confused. Most of the time our parents are/were disappointed, there was a vision that we did not know even existed. What if they had just told us what they expected from us? At that point, we had the opportunity to use their ideas or to use their ideas to shape our own or tell them that we are not able to use their ideas at all.

That transparency solves so much. It could have saved so much trouble, pain, and anxiety. Be honest so that your standards for her are different from your son(s).

What does she want? Can you agree to that? Why or why not? Share that with her. She needs to know. She may not have a long—term vision for the plan that she has. Help her to develop that plan into one you can support. This is key to your relationship. Her success is what allows you to sleep at night and have peace in your life.

Strategy.

Plan.

Execute as a unit.

Tell her the why behind your vision for her. Make sure you tell her when you failed at your plans, why you failed, and ultimately, tell her why it is important for her not to fail. Then reassure her that the world will not end if she does.

Help her construct a strategy to reach the goals. The strategy includes teaching her how to network, make connections, and how ask people for what she needs without having to ask.

Plan how and when to implement each stage of the strategy. Reevaluate the plan to make any necessary adjustments so that she can remain successful. She needs your leadership and guidance.

Show her how to evaluate the process and how to determine if she is successful. Show how to reach the top of her career and path.

Share why this is important

Risk it all and elevate her respect for you and her trust for you. Tell her your why. Why do you need her to be successful? Why does she need your help?

Why did you fail? What did you do to start over? What did you do to sacrifice for her success?

Tell her everything.

Expose your life.

Tell her all of the gory details.

Remind her of your investment in her and her life.

Remind her that she is your report card.

Teach her what the world does not want her to know.

## YOUR PROTECTION OF HER—YOUR SHOTGUN

When I speak to men about having daughters, they can agree that they are afraid for their fate because of how they treated someone else's daughter when they were younger—by a day or decades.

I tease them about owning or buying new shotguns. They may not buy the weapon and will never shoot anyone, it just makes them feel better that they could. It just made them feel better to say that they could shoot someone if they needed to.

Your protection of her is very important. She needs to know that you will protect her at all costs. She will want to know that you will defend her and come to her rescue when she needs help and support. You will want to help her establish her defense mechanisms and methods to save herself.

She should consider self—defense classes for her personal, and physical protection. That will be your recommendation and will only happen with your encouragement.

Now, she is going to meet someone who may be the love of her life. Please handle this well. This will not be like the young man who tried to date her from high school through college and even beyond will not be the same as the call that she makes when she tells you that she wants to meet someone special. She will be excited to share him with you. She is also asking for your approval. This will mean the world to her. Both of them need to know that you are on her side.

There's a shirt that reads: 10 Rules for Dating My Daughter

1. Get a job.
2. Understand that I don't like you.
3. I'm everywhere.

4. You hurt her, I hurt you.
5. Be home 30 minutes early.
6. Get a lawyer.
7. If you lie to me, I will find out.
8. She's my princess, not your conquest.
9. I don't mind going back to jail.
10. Whatever you do to her, I will do to you.

There's another one that reads: 'I have a backyard, a shovel, and an alibi.'

These are quite strong statements for protecting her. She needs to know it and feel it so that she can function in the world.

Sometimes, she needs you to protect her from herself.

Her mate selection will be based on you and your character traits. She will compare him to you all of the time, both mentally and verbally.

Share with her how to make this relationship work. Show her how to understand him. She will need some navigational support. Hold her accountable for her part—she is not always right when they have problems. She needs to understand that you are not always going to take her side.

She will need to be held accountable for participation in the success as well as the issue in that relationship. Make her work. Show her now.

# PERFECT RELATIONSHIP BY DESIGN

What do you feel is the perfect relationship?

Just some ideas are:

- Time well spent
- Deep conversations
- Lively debates
- Healthy competition
- Advice seeking
- Answering the questions
- Listening
- Trust
- Keeping confidences
- Remembering the details
- Protection
- Educational
- Invested
- Guiding
- Leadership
- Travel
- Strategy
- Dependable
- Independent
- Dreams
- Focus on the greatness of the relationship
- Teach her to overcome her failures
- Affirm her greatness

- Affirm her so that she overcome her fears
- Keep her close

This is no perfect relationship. Make it the best that you can.

*In Your Hands*

# WHO IS SHE?

## WHO DOES SHE THINK SHE IS?
## HOW DO YOU DESCRIBE HER?
## HOW DOES SHE DESCRIBE HERSELF?

She will be answering that question for the rest of her life, with varying answers and varying degrees of that answer. It is similar to the survey answers with offer extremely satisfied, somewhat satisfied, just satisfied, somewhat dissatisfied, and extremely dissatisfied. This will take place internally and externally, peacefully and rambunctiously. Sometimes all at the same time.

She will grow. She will change. She will vacillate between liking and disliking herself for the rest of her life. No one will have more influence over her than you. Not even her mother or future mate has more influence than you.

What will you help her learn about herself? What will you help her adjust about herself? What will you do to help her figure herself out? Can she figure out some of her issues with minimal support from you as she gets older?

Who she thinks she is is going to become and who she is not going to be a reality unless you intervene in some areas and oversee some other areas. If she develops a negative self—image, you can counteract that image through affirmations, coaching, and love. And time.

When you describe her, what do you say? The apple of your eye? The beat of your heart? The baby? The pumpkin? Whatever affectionate name you use to refer to her, remember that she has to grow to fill that title/role. She does not always feel that she is that young lady/woman that you believe that she is. There are times when she will not believe in the faith that you have in her. She does not always trust herself to be the young lady that you love and believe in. Keep affirming her. Remind her of tangible examples of her proving that to herself. She does not understand unconditional love yet, because there are so many other entities where she has to prove her worth. Everything that she experiences with these entities costs her something (school, home, siblings, friends), but then there's you, where love, time, and attention cost her nothing. It is conflicting and confusing. Again, share—your rationale and philosophy so that she can understand.

Her description of herself will change over time. Just check it frequently so that you can refine it as necessary.

*In Your Hands*

# WHO ARE YOU?
## WHO DOES SHE SEE?
## HOW DOES SHE DESCRIBE YOU?

Hero.

Champion.

Leader.

Guide.

Instructor.

Mentor.

She sees the perfect man like her dad. Unfortunately, you have to be perfect and you are not afforded any errors or mistakes. It is unfortunate, but she holds to the standard of EXCELLENT. With no reprieve. Without the possibility of forgiveness. At least not immediately.

That is what she sees. She will judge what you do. She is watching your every move. She wants to be sure that is not missing anything. She will be your shadow. Your mini-me. Your audio tape recorder—recording to repeat what she hears. Your video recorder—recording to repeat what she sees.

So, who are you? Are you proud of that image? Do you want her to repeat that? If not, then change. Now, does she know that she is not to follow you as an example? No, she does not. On the contrary; she fully expects to follow you. You are her leader, her tour guide, and her due north. She can't make those types of decisions. You need to be the person who she can depend on and trust, follow and whose information she can repeat, share and reuse. You don't have the option to take a break, a vacation, or quit. This is a full—time, 24 hours, 7 days a week, 365 days a year, no breaks, no vacations, no quitting, no appreciation, no praise, no raise, and no applause to do the right thing as your job as Dad. You are in an interesting position because you cannot afford to lose. Winning is the only option.

You are going to make some mistakes, some errors, some missteps, but you too have to recover from that immediately. She needs you at your best at all times. You don't have time for personal crisis or uncertainty.

You determine what she says about you and how true that is.

She should be able to brag about you. Girls who can brag about their dads have healthy self—esteem. She wants to be able to say that 'my dad will take me,' 'my dad will bring me,' and, 'I love my dad.' There are areas of dependability that she needs to be able to depend upon for her safety and security.

One daughter calls her father UberDad because he drives her and all of her friends to events before she had a car and was able to drive herself. All of her friends and teammates love and respect, honor, and cherish him for extending himself to her and her friends.

Who you are to her defines who she is for herself. When she decides what you do for her and who you are to her, she is secure and she feels loved. Those two facts enhance her self—esteem. That is essential to her growth as a woman.

Remember who you are. Remember who she is to you. Remember who you are to her.

## TEAM DADDY DAUGHTER

You are a team! Team Daddy—Daughter! You are on the same team. Following the same rules. She learns what she knows from you.

I learned about football from my father. He taught me the rules and I shared his love for the game. We also shared fanship in two teams.

You are a team—an alliance.

Consider what happens on a team. You are one. You live by the same life philosophy and code. The concern is that you understand that you teach that team concept.

You are her life partner. She depends on you for instruction. When you teach her to be a partner and helper and teammate, then this goes a long way for her work life, and her home life, now and in the future.

Teamwork is difficult to teach but showing it to her is the best method.

When she needs to talk and vent, share and argue. She needs to be able to share in a safe place that only her father can provide.

Teach her what it means to be dependable. Teach her what it means to be trusted and on the side of someone that you love. Be on her team. Teach her to be on yours.

Teach her to communicate like a team. Teach her the benefits of being a team member.

*In Your Hands*

# YOUR RELATIONSHIP WITH HER MOTHER

What is your relationship with her mother?

Married?

Divorced?

Never married?

Amicable?

Failed?

Respectable?

Reputable?

Whatever your relationship is and however you feel, please treat her mother well. Whew! There I said it. No matter what she has done, treat her well.

Your daughter will learn two (2) things when you do:

1) How she should be treated and respected by a man.

2) How to overcome conflict and resolve to co-exist.

These are two very valuable lessons for a daughter. You need to be instrumental in making sure that the relationship is preserved. Some of their issues will have nothing to do with you. Some of their issues will have EVERYTHING to do with you.

Initiate group decisions about her future, her present, and her life overall. She is the product and some of the two of you. She needs to hear from both of you. Sometimes that means at the same time and in person.

Help her—as best you can—to understand her mother. She needs your help to get along with her. As little girls, they may have been close, however, as a teenager, they may move apart. This change would be subtle or it could be World War 3. At this point, she will need your help to restore that relationship.

Help her to relate to her mother, pointing out similarities and positive attributes, so that she does not consider them so different that they can never come together and be a great mother-daughter unit.

Help her to understand the why behind her mother's behaviors and attitudes, words, and deeds. This translation will keep them closer rather than apart.

This is the key to some of the best peacemaking ever. Help her understand your 'why' as well. This helps her to make better decisions now and later.

No matter what she believes or wants to be true, she will need that relationship at some point. Both of you will want that relationship to be readily available to her.

Help them maintain a certain level of relationship, respect, rapport, and decorum. It may not be your responsibility but it is an asset to you. If you consider that if they have a good relationship, then you will have a certain level of peace. This relationship benefits you. It makes your job easier.

## HER RELATIONSHIP WITH HER MOTHER

This can be a great relationship or a terrible one or every step in between.

As mentioned in the previous chapter, help them so that they can not only survive each other but make a great historical moment and get along.

Teach her how to communicate with her mother. Keep coaching her on how it is most effective to talk to her about difficult topics, how to plan for her needs, how to best be forgiven, and how she celebrates.

Help her to invest in that relationship so that she will have her mother in her corner. It is easier to have her mother in her corner than it is to not have her.

Some mothers abandon their children and if there is no chance of saving the relationship, then help her to survive that abandonment.

Help her to maximize that relationship because of the magnitude. You don't want her to miss out on the wisdom that most mothers offer to their children.

Remind her of why you love(d) her mother. She needs to know about your story, especially if it was a love story. Or why it was not.

Your relationship with her mother may be a prelude to her future relationship. What do you want that to look like? How can you equip her to be able to make a relationship functional, great, and long-lasting?

What can you do to make sure that she succeeds and that she does not fail in her future relationships, and ultimately, her marriage? She needs to understand how to make this relationship work.

She needs to practice at home what is expected in the real world and it starts with her mother and you.

Apologize for any hurt you caused her or her mother. She needs to hear and feel that you are remorseful for all that you have done or not done. Help her heal—both of them. You have the tools and the influence and the ability. Use them to make a bridge for reconciliation.

## HER SELF—ESTEEM

Her self—esteem revolves around your feelings and reactions.

Self—esteem defined by Gage is how she feels about herself, how high she can hold up her head, and how much time we spend correcting her self—image.

You will need to do self—checks on her self—esteem regularly, weekly, or every two weeks. She needs to know that you are checking on her. She needs to know that she is accountable to you and she will know that you are paying attention.

Fewer girls commit suicide or self—harm when they are not allowed to be ignored or to fly under the radar.

Don't fall for 'fine' and 'okay.' Be sure that you don't ignore the signs that she needs you.

My father and stepfather both asked me daily how I was doing. They stopped and waited for an answer—a real answer.

So how does she feel about herself? How will you know exactly how she feels about herself? Why does she feel that way? If she does not feel good about herself, then how will you influence the improvement of her self—esteem?

Her self—esteem affects her courage to apply for employment, her ability to be completely engaged in her life, her wisdom about relationships, her desire to be great, and her integrity regarding her feelings.

These are important factors in her life, that you need to help guide and manage.

## HER IMAGE

Her image depends on you. What she wears and what she won't wear depends on the expected judgment from you.

As we consider the definition of an image, please remember that your definition is one that she uses to make her decisions. Image is defined by dictionary.com as a physical license or representative of a person. Additionally, the image is what she appears to be in public.

Her image is a reflection of you. Either she dresses in a manner that makes you proud or totally embarrasses you.

If her dress is too short or too sheer, then that will be reflected in how you shared with her how to dress and how carry herself.

You need to be direct when sharing how long her shorts should be, how opaque her shirt should be, and the rules of hair and other accessories.

Some fathers do not like her to change her hair so be honest. All of your rules may not be followed, however, make sure that she understands what those non-negotiables are so that you don't have friction. Her image leads to others judging her—sometimes, judging you as well.

The real matter of the image is the self—esteem and self—respect associated with that image known as dressing. Be honest with her about why there is a double standard. Offer alternatives so that she does not feel slighted about her modest dressing expectations.

Help her to feel good about herself.

What do you approve of? How will she know? What do you disapprove of? How will she know? Remind her those pictures are permanent. Those pictures could be used to deny her the ability to teach or to be confirmed as a US Supreme Court Justice.

This is a good time to discuss the scantily—clad bathroom selfies, which are usually sent to the current boyfriend. Some girls have done this and lived to regret it. One, in particular, shared a picture that was found on a pornographic site and she was shamed into no longer going to school. You need to spend some time talking to her about keeping her body covered while on camera and on social media. She will accuse you of being overprotective. She is correct. Tell her that it is true. Then tell her why.

Visit with her about these matters of image. Once it is out there, there is no taking it back.

## HER HEALTH

Hereditary. Learned. Earned. Owed.

Her health comes from you (and her mother)! What does she need to be cautious of? Some health concerns are hereditary, so what can she do to make sure that she does not expose herself to that condition(s)? So you have diabetes, caution her about her sugar intake and her diet patterns.

What does she eat? How often do you cook together? How often do you eat together? What does she know about nutrition? What do you do to enhance her attitude toward great nutrition?

You need to intentionally work toward helping her improve her diet by learning, then teaching her to eat well, avoid toxic ingredients, and drink plenty of water. Her water intake should be half of her body weight in ounces. So if she weighs 150 pounds, then she needs to drink 75 ounces of water each day.

Cook with her. Eat with her. Study nutrition with her. Reward her for doing what she should. Do it with her—both of you could improve, so do it together. Start today!

Her weight will change if she improves her diet. Paired with exercise, she is certain to change her body structure. If she is overweight, then she should lose some weight. When this happens, she will start to improve her self—esteem and her self—worth.

Exercise with her. Walk. Bike. Lift weights. Run. Play the sports that you all share. Yoga.

Teach her good practices and habits and make sure that she exercises regularly.

## HER WEALTH AND FINANCIAL WORTH

Her wealth and financial worth are not dependent on others. Money is different now and a difficult topic, but it is necessary to learn, understand, and execute.

What is the definition of worth? Financial worth is how much money one can earn or amass, save and invest at the time. This paper chase will last her whole life. I am sure that you are already familiar with this and may have already helped her to prepare at some level.

Remember that she is looking at the lifestyle that you enjoy and provide. Will she know how to reach and maintain that same level? Without your consistently supplementing that budget?

One dad was angry that his graduating daughter did not know what a money order was, much less what to do with it. That was a classic case of not teaching. She had never seen one because he does not use them to pay his bills. He uses online banking. When she calls for money, he transfers that money through an app before the phone call is over. She had not been the inside of a bank—not even to open an account that she is having the money transferred into. After explaining to the dad that she was born with a debit card in her hand, he then had to realize that he had not taught her this and then realized that they had grown up quite differently, starting with technology. He apologized to his daughter and took her to the bank the next day to deposit it into her account.

Keep in mind that she needs to learn and that education is your responsibility. How many bank accounts should she have? Checking. Savings. Money market. Investments. How many credit cards should she have? Two to three? What are your financial rules? How much should she never spend in her account? How much cash should she keep on hand? What is the minimum in the savings account? How will she start investing? When? How much?

She learns from your behavior. What you do is what she will do.

Teach her. Show her. Recommend your trusted advisors. Help her to see your vision for her. Help her to see as far into the future that you see.

Recognize the value of this education and what it will save you in the long run. You do not want to have to fund her lifestyle into adulthood because you were too busy to teach her how to pay bills, save, and manage her overall financial well—being.

## HER VALUE AND WORTH

What is her value? What is her worth? What is she worth to herself? What is she worth to others? This is very vague in certain instances, however, she needs to understand how to understand her value and worth. This translates into how to be valued at home, at work, and in her social circles.

Does she volunteer her talents to the right audience? Does she charge for her talent to the correct audience? What does she do to be valuable but she is undervalued? How can we help her to manage her worthwhile remaining humble and approachable?

## HER SPIRIT/SPIRITUAL BEHAVIOR

Her spirit, her soul, is a critical piece of who she is and how she manages what she takes into her spirit. What is she listening to? What does she read? What is she thinking about? What does she need to keep a functioning spirit? How can you help her with a healthy spirit?

Her spirit cannot be in jeopardy and could not be allowed over enemy lines. Her spirit needs to be strong and guarded so that she can reject issues and situations that she will face and address as she grows up. She will have to address these issues, so she needs to be able to address the issues which will she will face daily.

Help her to address issues honestly so that she will maintain her mental healing, without having to keep your secrets which is not her responsibility. She needs to be free of the family secrets and the associated weight with these secrets.

Her spirit needs to be protected and built so that she can withstand the spiritual attacks which she needs to withstand.

When she fails and falls for the attacks, how can you help her to recover from that? Some of the devastations will be minor and others will be major. She will need to recover from these various, surprising circumstances.

Help her to maintain the strong spirit which you are grooming within her and help her to recover from any faltering spirit incidents.

**HER LOVE**

How do we learn to love? By observation and experience is how. She will credit you with her education on love.

She defines love as time. You define love in other ways. She needs to expand her definition but not dismiss her original definition. She will eventually add investment, patronage, flattering, and reciprocity to her definition of love, but for now, her definition of love revolves around time.

She is going to watch you carefully and critically, judiciously, and analytically. She will use her findings to determine what she should do, AND what she should NOT do.

She will develop this definition and she will use this definition for the rest of her life. Please be okay with it because otherwise it will later embarrass you and disappoint you. You want her love to be successful. You want her to use what works for you but does not work for her until you realize that she needs a working definition for her with your approval.

You will be amazed by your influence over her love life. She will use phrases like, 'my dad will like you,' or 'you are going to love my father,' 'my dad is not going to like him,' and then, 'Dad, I have someone that I want you to meet.'

Be prepared to equip her to be a loving mate and a great lover. Teach her all that she needs to know about the man of her dreams and how to treat him and when to do so. Help her to distinguish between the man of her dreams and a mistake that she might make.

You shape her ability to love. She started by loving you first. She wants someone to love her just like you love her and then some.

When she is old enough to be married and to be someone's lover, she will need more lessons. This time as a lover. Your head is about to explode—right now. However, she will need your guidance in this area. You don't need to let her rely on her friends or the internet or that man to teach her how to be a great lover to the man that she loves.

Help her to make sure that she understands the body language and the mixed signals of men. Share with her the juicy and bitter details of what she will encounter. Share with her how to be the woman of any man's dreams while being her authentic self—make sure that she knows who that is.

You will shape who loves her. She will measure each man against you and your standards, your behavior, and your abilities. There is a mental checklist in each woman and she uses it to determine how that man will fit into her life. Before you meet him, he will need to have about 75% to 80% of that list mastered. You shape her present and future, which I am sure that you already know but may not have considered completing magnitude.

Help her to know when to walk away. There are times when she makes a selection mistake, at which point she may need help walking away. Please teach her when to walk away. Please teach her to walk away and how. Then be available to hear the recap of the relationship. She may cry but you will be there to listen to her, wipe her tears, and reaffirm her as a woman.

## HER EYES

The eyes are the window to her soul. The eyes don't lie and they are very revealing. They expose hurt and love, anxiety and excitement, danger and thanksgiving, disappointment and celebration. They tell the WHOLE story. Pensive. Penetrating. Elicit. Elusive. Kind. Loving. Dreamy. Dedicated. The eyes tell it all.

You need to keep those eyes glimmering and bright. You will want to keep the darkness away as well.

Look into them intentionally from time to time so that you can see the depths of her eyes, which is a hint of what is going on in her head.

Don't go too many days without looking into those eyes. She needs to be looked at and you need to do the looking.

What have they seen—her eyes? What do you recall that she has seen that should cause you concern? That she regrets seeing? That you regret? Protect her eyes. Rectify what you know that she saw that you regret. Her eyes are important. They are vulnerable when they are reflecting on what she is thinking and feeling, what she needs and wants. What she is concerned about and what she is considering.

What does she see? What do you want them to see? What are you showing her?

How are you shaping her eyes? What do you shield her from? How do you protect her eyes? How do you correct the things that she sees that you did not intend for her to see?

How do you share with her that her eyes have value? How do you share with her that her eyes have worth? How do you share with her that her eyes have energy? How do you share with her that her eyes have unlimited potential? How do you share with her that her eyes have answers? How do you share with her that her eyes have questions?

Her eyes tell the entire story. Help her shape and craft that story. Teach her how to overcome the issues which you regret her witnessing. Protect her eyes.

**HER EARS**

What does she hear? What has she heard? What does she listen to?

Challenge her on her music choices. This may mean changing your playlist. Listening to dark music facilitates a dark place.

What has she heard? Is she hearing negative words? Is that negative energy bouncing around inside of her creating more negative space?

What are her ears playing on repeat in her head? The negative or the positive? What of that do you guide and regulate? What if that did you miss the opportunity to stop and prevent it? What of that can you correct right now?

Research states that when one sense is weakened then the others become sharper. So, if the eyes take a break, then the ears sharpen up or the nose or the taste or maybe the touch. Whichever one is sharpest as the time is the primary sense. The goal is to keep them all sharp.

The ears hear. The mind remembers. The ears hear. The mind recalls. They compare to what they heard before to see if they have commonalities. The ear triggers a response.

Does she hear arguing and stress or love and forgiveness? What do you say to her? Are they words of power and praise? Are they critical and dogmatic? Are you affirming her? Are you reminding her of what she is made of? Are you thinking of her feelings and her well—being when you speak to her? Are you texting her daily words of affirmation and love? Are you sending her positive songs and motivating lyrics?

What can you do to add to her life through her ears?

Guard and protect her ears at all costs. Work on mitigating that outside noise such that she learns how to dismiss the negative noise which attempts to distract her from her path.

Help her to learn to dismiss those negative statements designed to wilt her self—esteem, even when it comes from close to home, from either you or her mother.

## HER MOUTH

This is an important instrument: her mouth. What will she do with her mouth? A woman is definitely and severely judged for what comes from her mouth. Her words are a reflection of everyone who she is associated with, which starts with you.

Help her to be judicious and responsible with her mouth and the words which she speaks. Remind her that the power of the tongue brings life as well as death. Consider sharing with her two examples of people whose words cost them opportunities with financial repercussions: Eddie Murphy and Kevin Hart.

Be transparent. Tell her what your irresponsible words cost you. Then, of course, be balanced. Share what words do well with your words.

Show her powerful words by famous people: Nelson Mandela, Nikki Giovanni, Martin Luther King, Jr., Barack, and Michelle Obama, John F. Kennedy, Marianne Williamson, important people: you, her mother, her grandparents, and your friends, and motivational people: your spiritual leader, her mentors, her teachers, and people that you want her to know.

Teach her to think before she speaks: that she cannot reel those words back in once they are out of her mouth. Make sure that she is thinking about the consequences of her words, what actions will result from her words, like did she hurt someone's feelings or pride, did she just end a career or a friendship, or did she cause someone to take their own life? Did she trust the wrong person with some sensitive information, whether her own or someone else's?

Sometimes we are not specific enough with our directions, advice, and idioms.

The next thing is to help to remember the consequence of a live microphone backstage. Some countless politicians and entertainers have said 'ugly' words when they thought no one was listening. If you cannot say it everywhere and you don't want it to be repeated, then you may want to reconsider if you should say it at all.

*In Your Hands*

The mouth is a product of her mind, heart, and soul—all that is inside. When her words are salty, sour, bitter, unrefined, terse, angry, malicious, hurting, hurtful, and/or dangerous then it is time for an inner wellness check. It is time for you to pull her over to the place where you talk to her and ask her what the problem is. You need to hear her speak and she needs you to listen to her speak, offer some advice and support, and then help her to solve the underlying problem.

What do the words she speaks offer to others? Power? Inspiration? Motivation? Her words need to offer something such as hope, motivation, or power. This may not be something she does at ten years old but she needs to have some direction and an intentional direction by graduation from college.

She will be known for her words, whether she realizes that or not. Her words. The sound of her voice. How do people feel after she closes her mouth? What do people think after she closes her mouth? She needs to know that her words have impact and meaning. Many of those words will resonate with people for years to come. Only she can determine what that message is and how it can transform the lives which she comes into contact with.

Her mouth will negotiate business deals, answer questions in class, call your name, argue about the price of a dress, call her to mate on the phone, say I love you, order food, scream while in pain, sing the love ballad of the year, teach a class, lead a workshop, pledge her vows, debate her points, and say words that will be cherished along with some she will regret.

You don't want her to sacrifice any part of her future because she is not judicious enough with her mouth.

Let us be clear and transparent. She needs to know that with the invention of the camera phone and internet, her words and actions for that matter can and will live on forever; those sound bites will live on forever. Some of which she may live to regret and which will hurt her future career. Unfortunately, she needs to be concerned about how she will feel if and when her children search for her on the internet. What will they think, feel and believe?

She dictates all of those narratives. She is in control of that by deciding what to do and being able to live with that decision. Female comedians with vulgar mouths have never attempted to be Supreme Court Justices. This is an extreme example but should shed some light on what the consequences are for our words.

They probably cannot be classroom teachers either. People will judge her character by her mouth. Condition her mouth for her future. Be willing to understand whatever position she chooses.

Limit your foul and unwholesome language. When children are small, they repeat what they hear within the context that they heard it. You don't want the teacher(s) to call you and tell you that your daughter said a foul word; the one that you inadvertently introduced last night when you screamed at a bad call at a football game. You did not think that she could hear you and didn't think that she would repeat it. And while at school. You are unrecoverably embarrassed.

Help her with her mouth by controlling yours. Advise others to do the same.

How do you respond to those incidents? How do you solve that situation? How do you undo what just happened? It is hard to explain that Daddy can do what his daughter will be punished for and will cause her shame and discount her worth.

Her mouth will challenge you.

Her mouth will impress you.

Her mouth will appall you.

Her mouth will rescue you.

*In Your Hands*

Her mouth will stop you.

Her mouth will make you reconsider your life.

Help her to shape that mouth's message. She needs that guidance. She cannot afford to be reckless with her mouth, especially if her decisions cannot be changed or altered in any way. Imagine what words would stall an otherwise promising political career.

Manage her mouth.

Mind her mouth.

Mute her mouth. When appropriate. Anytime she lacks the judgment to do so herself. Save her from herself.

Details that you cannot see trigger these words. Respond to 'incidents' immediately. Tactfully. Firmly. Wisely.

If anyone has to ask where her parents are, you are already late.

Even if she is grown, this is still your area of responsibility and concern.

How can you teach, advocate, advise, coach, supervise, direct, and lead this daughter and her mouth, which can be educated, sarcastic, and respectful all at the same time such that she does not self—sabotage the greatness ahead of her? Daily.

By being her dad.

## HER MIND

Her mental capacity increases over her lifetime. She has to remember the most between ages 6 to 18. Between home and school, she has to retain, learn, and process an immeasurable amount of information. This information is then used at various times without warning. The idiom 'her mind is steel trap' refers to a woman who does not forget anything and is very judicious about what she takes in and what she shares. You want her to be a woman with a mind which is a steel trap. However, that mind only becomes a steel trap with intentional training.

This training includes reading and practice. She needs to hear you train her brain to do what you want it to do. You want her to be intellectually savvy and wise and smart. This requires book sense. Common sense, logic, and street smarts. It is never too early to teach these skills. She needs the ability to read people in all situations to determine if she can trust her audience or determine if she is under attack.

She needs to be respected, even intimidating, so that only potential mates that understand how to respect her will approach her. These are complicated standards to reach but she needs all of them so that she does not fall victim to the prey that waits for gullible women.

Teach her to think like you so that she is equipped to overcome such issues. You have to use every day and every opportunity to make sure that she understands how to manage the tricks, and become successful without leaving a scorched path.

There is an idiom that states that you attract more bees with honey than with vinegar. That is a phrase that I definitely think could be rewritten. No one is attempting to attract stinging, life-threatening insects. Maybe we are trying to say that we are trying to relate to others who are not reasonable enough to handle communication. At any rate, it is focused on being nice to others in a professional manner which compels them to fulfill your requests.

Help her to think strategically. Many women are not strategists, resulting in uncalculated moves and unnecessary risks with result in more lessons, rather than success.

What is guiding her thinking? Her thought process? What is she reading? Watching? Who is she talking to? Her friends? Experts in her areas of interest? You have a vested interest in the exact answers to all these questions. Training excellence in the mind requires time and energy. You will need to give your undivided attention. What is on her mind? Your direction should be that she has only her present on her mind so that her future can unfold according to plan. This is not a coincidental situation. Everything that she achieves will be by design. She needs everything that she does to be focused on that purpose.

You need to program that steel trap with what she needs to know. She needs to remember what she learns, hears, reads, and knows so that her information is readily available for her use to advance her education and career.

Regarding her mind, there may be things which you may want her to forget: fights you have had with her mother, issues which she faced that were not favorable, accidents, incidents, pain and hurt. She needs to remove those negative experiences once she extracts the lessons. But you cannot let those negative experiences affect your daughter's thought process and mental wellness. She needs to remember all of the great experiences that she has encountered and use those experiences to remain motivated for what is ahead. She will encounter some painful days when this motivation will be needed, but she will need it so it needs to be there.

You shape her mind with your mental influence as well as your mental capacity. She needs you to help her elevate her mind so that she can expand her mind to the level that she can achieve all that she has on the list. You shape her study habits. You shape her mental intake.

Her mind has immense value. She needs to be reminded of that value and worth. From this day until the end of her days, she will be graded and judged on her mental abilities, her mental capacity, her mental status, and her mental prowess. She will use this mind for solving problems, solving issues for herself and others, for solutioning logistical issues, and assisting others with their life's work. Her mind needs to be respected so that she will be respected as she is hired, promoted, trusted, and makes money-making and life-changing decisions. She needs to be depended upon as an officer of a publicly-traded company or a privately held company. She will have access to spending a significant amount of the company's money and has the possibility of making significant decisions that could earn or lose the money for the company.

Her mind needs to be sharp and agile so that she can make solid decisions under pressure and with short processing times.

Her mind has value and worth. She needs to think and act as if she is aware of the high value and vast worth. She will need reminders from time to time.

You will need to ban certain words from her vocabulary: stupid, dumb, and any other words which contradict her intelligence, smarts, and brilliance.

She needs to know what is on your mind. She needs to watch you think, understand your thought process, understand the decision that you made based on the options that you had, and how you delivered that decision. This is usually learned on the job, at the moment, and will involve mistakes/learning. There are times when she cannot afford to learn. You need to show her inner workings of your mind.

What will she use as her mental anthem? She needs a mental anthem. This anthem will chime in when she has a moment of doubt, a moment of weakness, a moment of struggle, and when you are not available to give her the pep talk or motivational speech.

This mental anthem has to be chosen carefully. It is a transitional moment between staying on the path or steering away from it because of doubt or disbelief. This is chosen carefully because it is important for this motivational drive that the anthem infuses into her brain a start button that reminds her to charge ahead with fierceness and boldness, with bravery and courage.

While this anthem is important and necessary, she will need to change it from time to time. When her job titles change, home role changes or new influences enter her life, she will need to change or/and add to that anthem.

This anthem can be a statement, a song, or a video. Some examples of powerful songs are Survivor by Beyonce and Roar by Katy Perry. Statements such as the excerpt from Marianne Williamson's book address 'Our deepest fear is that we are not inadequate.' This excerpt is POWERFUL. The speeches by Dr. Martin Luther King, Jr., John F. Kennedy, and Nelson Mandela are some powerful, motivating words. Some quotes also provide motivation: "There is nothing to fear itself." by Franklin D. Roosevelt.

The videos are a quick motivational tool. Movie clips from Coach Carter, Finding Nemo, Akeelah, and the Bee, Remember the Titans, Hardball, and The Princess and the Frog are some great movies to find motivational moments. These are just a few of the great movies where good motivational moments can be found. Save them in your youtube.com playlist.

Selecting the anthem is critical because it is a motivational element. This anthem drives you to remember who you are, redirects you back to your path, and reminds you of your 'why.' This happens all under three (3) minutes. This is a quick jolt, not overly invasive. The anthem is a reminder of already established mental toughness and agility to accomplish the task(s) at hand.

Her mind can be the enemy's playground or scoreboard. She needs to be in control. She needs to be able to shift out of the negative voices and only hear the positive; she only needs to consult those who have her best interests and keep her whole.

Her mind is an important place and we need to keep it intact and keep it that way.

## HER HEART

The heart's value is defined by the understanding of her tenderness, kindness, compassion, empathy, and the ability to love other humans. Her heart houses the love, care, concern, and consideration she has for others. Her heart loves.

Her heart has very little protection. There is essentially nothing surrounding it which keeps the bad out and the good within. She is not built like you. Her heart and mind are in conflict regularly and the heart wins and the mind protests because there is no reasonable logic.

She needs to be able to love and so she is subject to the risk of a broken heart this is not limited to eros love but includes agape too. You could break or have already broken her heart. Her mother certainly has the capacity. Her friends may break her heart. How does she heal from that break of the heart? It is different healing process for each category, however, some heartbreaks are more difficult than others to recover and overcome.

She needs to be able to seek you for assistance in the processing of the matter of the heart as well as how to heal from the various types of hurt that she will encounter and eventually endure.

You will need to do frequent checks on that healing process. You will know if she heals completely (98%) and if she has not then you need to help her manage that pain and disappointment so that she does not externalize it nor keep it buried such that she is not bitter or broken.

You don't want her to quit on love. You don't want her to be bitter. You don't want her to be broken so that she is guarded and never realizes true love because she was still focused on her former issue.

You will need to help her to shape her heart in a manner that assists her to understand the nature of relationships, and most importantly how to ask the right questions and know that she can discern the truth of the answers, thus understanding if that person will be good to her and for her.

She needs to be able to understand your heart so that she can understand her own. She knows nothing until she learns the house rules of love and relationships.

One such rule is that she cannot date where she works. A second rule is that it is so much easier to walk away from a bad relationship if she does not have sex with him. Three, she needs to understand the mind of a man. Four, she needs to understand the heart of a man. Five, remember her worth so that she can remind others of the same.

Share your heart with her. Tell her who broke your heart. Tell her whose heart you broke. How did you heal? How did she heal? Tell her how to overcome that hurt and pain.

Her heart is worth protecting, saving, and healing. Her heart has value and worth. Your affirmations and encouragement make it possible to walk away from bad relationships; enable her to take a stand for herself; and, she is secure in her self—worth and self—esteem, confidence, and value. Her heart is whole and it needs to remain whole.

Her heart's wholeness has to last until she dies so that she can love her mate, her children, her family, her friends, and herself. She cannot love others if loving herself is so difficult or impossible.

Her heart is valuable. She needs to remember that. You need to remind her.

**HER ADVOCATE**

An advocate is defined as a person who speaks or writes in support or defense of a person or a course according to dictionary.com.

She needs an advocate—mentor so that she can be advised on matters which she needs advice and guidance about educational matters, and other matters that an outside source, such as a teacher or church member, can help her with.

This role is important because there are matters in which others have connections and expertise. We need them.

You shape this relationship by vetting the mentor, sharing the direction of the mentorship, and helping to hold her accountable. The mentor needs to be trustworthy.

The advocate will also affirm her as well as encourage her to achieve at exceptional heights. The mentor—a great one—repeats what you say but the presentations are different and she is not the parent. Your daughter will listen and will act on her advice. Trust the advocate until you can't.

## THE COMPETITION

You compete for her with people, gadgets, music, the internet, and details that you'll never know or understand. How does this happen? Well, you need to realize that you have competition and that competition will overtake you if you are not careful. It happens when new and shiny objects are introduced. She is interested because they are novel and mysterious to her. Now things include mates, gaming systems, cars, phones, alcohol, drugs, and fashion, to name a few.

The competition can override and challenge your voice. You will know that competition has arrived when her commentary leads with 'well, my friends did _ _____.' Don't misjudge the level of your competition. Your competition is designed to part you and your daughter.

Those elements steal your daddy/daughter's time and encourage her to challenge your knowledge and influence.

How do you overcome this competition? You will qualify some and disqualify others. You offer her an audience with a few and you disqualify the others. She needs to understand how to filter and sift through information. You need to teach her how to qualify the information and how to use well what she sees.

When she brings information to you, even if you don't want to hear it, LISTEN to her. ASK questions like 'where did you get that information from' and 'what is the source of that information.' Once she answers that question, then you can ask her why she trusted that information and why she wanted to use their information and advice. You need to know what her thoughts are and what she is going to do with that information.

After all of your questions and her answers, then you can walk through how to qualify and disqualify and disprove the information. She needs you to understand that she tried to seek some answers on her own and she is verifying the information.

She wants to make as few mistakes as possible. She wants you proud of her. She wants you to know that she was listening to all of what you said and that she understood all that you have shown her.

Teach her how to graciously reject bad advice and faulty information. Make sure that something that seems too good to be true probably is. Don't take any wooden nickel reinforces to not fall for schemes and scams. If the offer is only good for the next 15 minutes, then let it go. She needs to hear from you and see examples. You may never listen to the same music with your children and maybe you should not. There are songs that both of you will share. There will be remakes that you will share. Share them. Enjoy each other as you do so.

Judge your competition conservatively. Her mate is not your competition either actually. The mate does not want to take your place. The mate also wants our approval. Further, you will have to rectify their information. And sometimes that requires teaching both of them.

A dad took his daughter to buy a truck. The boyfriend had lots of information to contribute. After many looks of disdain, the daughter finally said to the boyfriend to stop talking and offering advice. The boyfriend wanted the father to know that he knew some things about buying a vehicle. The dad did not want to know that. That is not competition, but it was confirmation and it was complimentary. What the dad did not know was that the daughter told the boyfriend that her dad was impressed with men who had great credit and knew how to buy a vehicle. The boyfriend was trying to prove himself trustworthy to be awarded the title.

She wants to prove to you that she was listening to your lessons. She wants to prove that she was paying attention. If you do not listen to her, this is when you start to lose to the competition. We need to ensure that you do not fold to the challenges that she presents to you. Your behavior gives the 'competition' leverage over her. You cannot afford to let that happen. Keep focused on educating her. This investment separates and disqualifies the competition.

**WINNING HER BACK: SHE'S ACROSS ENEMY LINES**

Something bad happened. Something really bad. You have lost your power and influence over her life. She is across enemy lines! And you are surprised! And disappointed! Distraught! Amazed!

Enemy lines include but are not limited to drugs, pregnancy, low grades, social media, low self—esteem, low self—worth, identity crisis, missing school, or suicidal activities (such as cutting). She can be across enemy lines and be in your presence daily. She can be across enemy lines without giving you any indication.

Let's consider these levels of crisis separately. Pregnancy is not going to go well with you, but she still needs you. She needs your voice and your guidance and support. How does she move forward? How do you help manage that situation? What words will you use and what actions will you take to help her keep her self—esteem intact? What will you do? What won't you do? The difference is your behavior will be determined by how old she is. The younger that she is, the more challenges will be presented. But why was she having sex? Low self—

esteem is the usual reason for having sex as a middle school and high school student. So how do we adjust her self—esteem so that she can say no to sex? One word of advice: keep her talking. Ask her all of the questions so that you make her understand that you are still invested.

Low grades are also a symptom of low self—esteem. However, low grades will also be a signal that a drop—out could be in your future. Low grades are a signal for attention. Set goals for each grading cycle so that she can see the progress she makes. This also lets her know that you are paying attention. She will focus better when you know what is going on—it means that she matters.

Missing school means that she doesn't feel valued. Maybe she feels invisible. She thinks that no one is paying attention; that she won't be missed. You need to remind her of the contrary. Check her attendance. Email her teachers. Send lunch to her. Go eat with her. Send gifts to her during the day. Let her know that she is in a safe place. This is a great time to find an on-campus mentor who will check on her and with whom she can check in to share what is on her mind in real-time on campus and who can take real-time action on her behalf.

Identity crisis happens mostly between grades six and twelve. So this comes in many forms. Does she know her biological roots? Is she being raised by a relative and missing one or both parents? Is someone always asking her if she is 'mixed'? Is she defining herself as any member of the LGBTQIA community? How is she handling it? What did you say when she shared her feelings/choices? Did you embrace her or did you reject her? Remember that she had a choice to share or not. She chose to share. Don't squander that trust or investment. She needs your support in this particular season. This choice is not well received and she will be treated poorly, possibly discriminated against, and judged for the rest of her life. This can go poorly. There are statistics about how many girls attempt to or commit suicide after identifying with the LGBTQIA community. Ask her questions that you want to know. Don't just use the internet to find out the information and believe what you read. Further, don't blame yourself. Don't push her away with your own biases and concerns, judgments, and criticisms. This is a hard place to be for anyone. She needs someone who is in her corner, on her side, defends her, and listens to her when she speaks.

She needs your support to figure out who she is and what she wants.

Teachers know more about your child than you do because they spend more time with her. Teachers hear conversations that you want and don't want to hear. So, when you are suspicious of suicidal tendencies or activities, you need to consult her teacher(s). There are at least one thousand resources about suicide, detention, and education. The one tip for sure is to check for cutting on the arms, stomach, and legs. Be very concerned about hoodies in 80°F weather. That is indicative of cutting and sometimes intravenous drug use. As previously shared in communication, just ask if she has had suicidal thoughts. Again, listen to her. Believe what she says. Act on what you hear.

Suicidal thoughts must be stifled as soon as possible. This requires medical attention and immediate solution to the issues which cause these thoughts. Winning her back includes making hard decisions and unpopular arrangements. Take a stand for her.

Low self—esteem and low self—worth are closely related, however, both of them mean that she does not feel good about herself and does not feel worthy of anything significant. She does not look at herself in the mirror. She insults herself. She does not think that much if anything is positive about her. She does not believe in herself. She does not think that she is smart.

Low self—esteem translates into low self—investment, so she also cannot believe that others believe in her. So, she wonders why would someone believe in her. She does not even know what happened. You have the power to lift her out of her STUFF. She will need to be taught and coached into believing in herself. You may have done a great job helping her to build her self—esteem, however, there are some issues, which undermine your intentions, so you have to continually reinforce and reaffirm that self—esteem. I know that this is new for you that you have to keep saying, doing, and reinforcing the same influence within her life but you are not with her 24/7 and do not hear or see everything that she sees and hears. You will always have to overcome things that will wilt her self—esteem and sometimes you will not know what has happened. You only experience the results.

Drugs and alcohol! Tough subjects! Experimentation is the life of most teenagers. They will introduce each other to what they see, hear and read about. The problem is that these teenagers do not know the risks that they are taking can last their entire lifetimes. Tell her about the risks. If she still takes that risk, then at least she did so knowingly. Risks include being pre-exposed to hereditary addiction, the effect of other medications that she is prescribed and is taking, the random drug tests administered by athletic organizations, future political careers, including President of the United States or Supreme Court Justice of the United States or the FBI or other law enforcement agencies, or other entities which ask about drugs and alcohol usage or do testing.

Drug and alcohol experimentation is risky at best. There is not been a successful manner in which to do so. She is going to decide to try or not. So how do you feel more comfortable with that trial—and—error experiment? The consequences for you showing it to her under the age of 18 has a serious set of consequences, including the endangerment of a minor, so you put your career in jeopardy as well as your freedom. If she tries it with friends, she can be suspended from school, if done on or around campus. During this experiment, what if she dies? How are you sure that the drug is not laced with something deadly or an additive for future addiction? So, what are the rules for trying drugs? How do you start this conversation? What is permissible? What are off-limits? There are instances in which children have gotten drugs from their parents' rooms. How comfortable are you with her trying drugs from some adults that you don't know or some adults that you did not know did drugs? Realize that this happens. Children get drugs from their parents and then use those drugs and share those drugs with other children. Not sure that there is a winning and legal solution to any of this.

The effects are long-lasting. Alcohol is not different. There are parents which allow drinking at their home with the intent of hoping that they won't drink out with their friends. Research has shown that drinking at home and early does not deter drinking but rather encourages more drinking.

Again, what level of comfortability are you at for allowing your daughter to drink under supervision? The last thing you want is to be instrumental in your daughter being caught, or worse, addicted because she shared the experience so that no one else would.

Again, there is not an easy way to address this issue, but you need to consider your strategy. My father let me taste his beer. If she is ever addicted to anything, you have another issue: stop the addiction via rehabilitation. This is a long road to recovery and remaining sober. You never want her across these lines because you run the risk of never getting her back. And if you do, she will never be the same.

Social media is not the source of all evil, but it does start a good amount of trouble. Social media can put her across enemy lines. Girls have fought, scrapped, lied, and died because of what was done on social media. They have been bullied and been bullied on social media. They have exposed cheating mates and threatened to fight the person. All on social media.

Monitor her social media accounts. ALL of them. She has aliases, too. ALL of them. Watch what she says and what is being said to her. Know her friends and who are interested in her. Who is chatting with her? Is someone in her messages trying to meet her?

Request/require her passwords and login information. You need to be able to see what is happening with her. As she grows up, keep talking to her and asking her the questions which lead to answers about who she listens to and who is listening to her.

What is in that cell phone? As long as an adult is paying that bill, it is subject to inspection. LOOK! If you are honest, you did not grow up with a cell phone. They did not exist until 1986 but were expensive. They became affordable by 1994 and more plentiful. The first smartphone was produced in 1994. The first phone to take pictures was produced in 2000.

Your daughter was born into the cell phone industry. She got one as soon as you decided that she could have it. She did not have to wait until it was created or available. Similar to the debit card scenario, you have to teach her how to best use that very powerful device that she holds in her hand all day, every day. Part of the best use means that you have to manage your expectations and her behavior. There was a story about a young lady who was a junior in high school. She was dating a young man to whom she sent pictures of herself in the bathroom mirror. Some of these pictures—the ones that they showed on television—were of her in her bra and panties. Others were not able to be shown on television but were found on pornographic sites. The discovery rendered her devastated. She not did survive the ridicule and the sneers so she stopped going to her high school and was homeschooled, missing prom and graduation. When the show host interviewed her, she mentioned the companion promised not to share the pictures with anyone, however that did not seem to be true. The heartbreaking story of a girl trying to impress and keep a boyfriend happy turned out so much more harmful than expected. This is going to be her story forever.

That cannot be removed from the internet and eventually, she may have children.

So that you don't have any future issues, please inspect her phone for photos and have a serious conversation about the photos that she takes and those that she sends. Further, discuss what she allows others to photograph.

This is YOUR daughter. TELL her the 'game' of young men so that she is prepared to say NO to these schemes. How will you feel if your daughter's photographs are found on a porn site? Seen by your friends? Co-workers? Church members? Supervisor? Your breath just quickened. Your heart just leaped out of your chest. So talk and search the phone. Give her the courage to say no to such things. Forgive her if there are already pictures.

You need to win her back. Just because she is growing and when she is grown, you don't give your title and your role. It may be modified and will look different at every turn but your words, your wisdom, your investment, and your love is always necessary.

She may not be happy with your tactics and techniques but she will respect you and she will share that respect with others.

You will know when you have won her back when despite her growth and brownness, she shares all of the details as she once did. She is reminded to trust you and she remembers what she is worth.

Get her back from across enemy lines AND never let her return!

# The Power of the Daddy/Daughter Relationship

Dear Kylie,

    Upon your arrival, all I could think of is how my baby girl will be here any day now. As I got that call from your mother it seemed as time didn't move as I flew down the freeway to be the first to see you for the first time. Getting closer, the flood of thoughts ravages my brain of tea parties, dance battles, Father & Daughter dances, date nights, and so much more. Once I put my eyes on you, all I could think was those days couldn't come any faster. Baby Doll, stay courageous, live life, you only have one, so cherish the little things. Yes, life will bring you up at one time and take you down at the best of times but remember these three letters. BCC: Bold -Calm -Confident. Be Bold, Stay Calm, Remain Confident.

Daddy always loves you!!!

Kyron J. Gage, Sr.

## GUMBO

Job descriptions that you have because you are her dad.

Mediator

Advocate

Teacher

Keep those roles in front of each of you. She needs that.

Help her to understand her womanhood. She needs to understand its power. She needs to learn to use it in proportion to the situation that she faces. Remind her to never threaten something that she never intends to carry out. Threats make her unbelievable. She won't be taken seriously.

Remind her that she needs to restrict those who can help redefine or/and refine the woman that she is.

She is a whole human. She does not need to be completed by anyone. She is complete already.

## THE DADS WHO DO THIS WELL

You need your own mentor! Who parented well? Your dad? Your grandfather? Your pastor? Whomever it was, call him and ask him for advice now and forevermore.

You will need another father to give you fatherly advice about being a great father.

Meet with him monthly. Listen to his stories. Ask questions. Heed his advice. Share your concerns. Hear his advice. Take action.

This is very valuable to you.

There is a show released in 2020 called the Council of Dads. Watch the pilot. It was a great show.

# THE DADDY/DAUGHTER SCHEDULE

You need a standing appointment with your daughter.

Date night—at least once each month.

Decide on which events you will attend together.

What happens when you spend time together?

Rule #1: Don't ever break that date for anyone else unless someone is hospitalized and she would be going as well.

Rule #2: Device-free except for Daddy/Daughter selfies.

Cherish these moments. All of them matter. All of them count. All of them matter. Don't take one of them for granted. Next time is NOT guaranteed.

When she goes away or is away, video conferencing is key to the relationship. Need to put your eyes on her.

## YOUR OTHER RELATIONSHIPS

Do you protect this relationship like you protect your other relationships? With zeal and might? With fervor and fierceness?

Make sure that all of your other relationships understand the importance of your relationship with your daughter. Do not sacrifice it for any reason.

Some men make this mistake when they remarry. Some men make this mistake when they date. Please do not take this relationship for granted and do not sacrifice it for anyone.

She gets one dad.

Protect that relationship with ALL of your being. She is your report card. This relationship deserves all of your energy. You cannot hold her accountable if you have not laid the groundwork as her dad.

## IN YOUR HANDS

You hold her self—esteem in your hands. Be bold. Be great. Be her hero. Be the man in her life. She needs you.

I know that this is a lot, however, it's what you need to know so that you can give her what she needs.

# Acknowledgments

God, thank You for Your plans for me. Thank You for **In Your Hands: A Dad's Impact on His Daughter's Self-Esteem** and for choosing me to complete Your project with the words that come out of my mouth. I just want to please You. Thank You for continuing to anoint me and to invest in me and my gifts, which keep surprising me. Thank You for loving and forgiving me.

Jordan and Nehemiah, thank you for supporting me and my endeavors. Thank you for loving me, especially when I do nothing without a pen and a clipboard, thank you for enduring my late nights, your ideas, the sounding board, the love, and the support. Thank you for celebrating our legacy.

To my prayer partners and my accountability partners, thank you for the long talks, the powerful prayers, and the encouragement. To my pastor and church family, thank you so much for your love and support.

Onedia N. Gage speaks from experience as a Daughter. She wants you to know the power of your impact. The native Houstonian misses her father, step-father, and grandfathers every day. Be the dad that your daughter will miss when you leave this earth. It is well worth whatever you have to overcome in order to achieve the success.

Please feel free to contact me and share your feedback. onediagage@onediagagespeaks.com, or @onediangage (twitter). www.onediagagespeaks.com
Blogtalkradio.com/onediagage
Youtube.com/onediagage10
Facebook.com/onediagage

## CONFERENCE SPEAKER ♦ WORKSHOP LEADER

To invite Dr. Gage to speak at your event,

Please contact us at: www.onedigagespeaks.com

@onediangage (twitter) ♦ onediagage@onediagagespeaks.com ♦ facebook.com/onediagage

youtube.com/onediagage ♦ blogtalkradio.com/onediagage ♦ ongage (Instagram)

## **Publishing**

Do you have a book you want to write, but do not know what to do?
Do you have a book you need to publish but do not know how to start?
Would publishing move your career forward?

Let us help
onediagage@purpleink.net ♦ www.purpleink.net
**281.740.5143**